SON OF
MUSCLE CAR MANIA

MORE ADS 1962-74

MITCH FRUMKIN

Motorbooks International
Publishers & Wholesalers Inc

Osceola, Wisconsin 54020, USA

© Mitch Frumkin, 1982

ISBN: 0-87938-154-X
Library of Congress Catalog Card Number: 82-3527

Printed and bound in the United States of America.

1 2 3 4 5 6 7 8 9 10

Cover illustration by Mitch Frumkin.
Cover design by William F. Kosfeld.

Motorbooks International books are also available at discounts in bulk quantity for industrial or sales-promotional use. For details write to Marketing Manager, Motorbooks International, P.O. Box 2, Osceola, Wisconsin 54020.

Library of Congress Cataloging in Publication Data

Frumkin, Mitch, 1943-
   Son of muscle car mania.

   1. Automobiles—Miscellenea. 2. Automobiles—
Pictorial works. I. Title.
TL15.F743   629.2'222'0973   82-3527
ISBN 0-87938-154-X (pbk.)   AACR2

Son of Muscle Car Mania

Preface

Son of Muscle Car Mania continues the "Mania" tradition in presenting another 250 high-performance car ads.

This second volume begins two years earlier than the original book, with some of the 1962 models, and takes you up to the gas lines of 1974.

This book includes automobiles not covered before, such as the turbocharged Avantis and the letter series Chrysler 300's. The Shelbys, Road Runners, etc. are, of course, all back with more imaginative artwork and gutsy slogans—each proclaiming the superiority of its fire-breathing models.

I've included, as in the first volume, at least one source where the avid enthusiast can locate the actual full-size ads.

Monster horsepower cars were strictly an American phenomenon that most likely will never happen again. So, let loose of those mpg blues and experience through these ads a time when muscle cars ruled.

Mitch Frumkin
April 1982

**To all Frumkins
past, present and future . . .
especially my sons David & Kristian**

Contents

Chapter One
American Motors

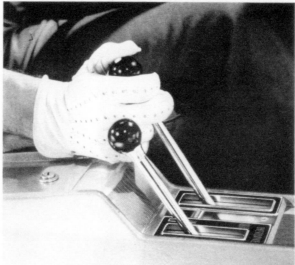

MOTOR TREND: JANUARY '63. AMERICAN MOTORS SLOWLY JOINED THE MUSCLE MANIA WITH ITS 270-HP ENGINES AND TWIN-STICK TRANSMISSIONS.

How to pick a new '64 Rambler just for the sport of it

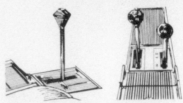 

Choose one of 7 transmissions. New Shift-Command floor stick, optional on V-8's, is fully automatic, or you shift it. Other options include sports-action Twin-Stick Floor Shift.

Select from Six or V-8 powerplants. New Classics offer choice of economical Sixes or spirited 198-hp V-8. Ambassadors are powered with a 250-hp V-8, 270 optional.

Pick slim or wide bucket seats from widest choice of seat options. Both types recline to 5 positions—move back or forward for individual legroom comfort. Optional adjustable headrests for front seats help you relax, protect against whiplash injury.

Add an Adjust-O-Tilt Steering Wheel This all-new optional feature adjusts to 7 positions for easier entry and exit, most comfortable driving position.

Wrap it all up in slick new Rambler '64 styling, add extra values like Advanced Unit Construction, Deep-Dip rustproofing, many more—and you have terrific buys in these new '64 Ramblers!

The all-new Ambassador V-8 wagon

The all-new Classic 770 hardtop 6 or V-8

FREE! '64 CAR X-RAY BOOK! 32 illustrated pages comparing the leading '64 cars. At your Rambler dealer.

Insist on more in '64—go Rambler

Rambler American • Rambler Classic 6 or V-8 • Rambler Ambassador V-8

65-990

'65 Rambler Ambassador— spectacular wherever you look

Spectacular new engine choices— Sensible Rambler economy

Big V-8 options, up to 327 cu. in. New Torque Command 232, the Six that comes on like an Eight, standard.

Spectacular sporty options— Sensible personalized comfort

New reclining buckets, console, manual or automatic floor shifts are optional. Roomiest, most luxurious Rambler ever.

Largest and Finest of the all-new Ramblers for 1965, the totally new Ambassador is longer by nearly a foot; wider, with more room than ever for passengers and luggage. Sparkling with twice as many entirely new models, including the stunning new convertible above, hardtops, sedans and wagons. New engine choices that start with the world's most advanced Six, go up to V-8 options of 287 or 327 cu. in. And you can customize your Ambassador exactly as you like it, with options such as All-Season Air Conditioning, wire-wheel covers, headrests, anti-roll heavy-duty springs and shocks—the works. All have the famous Rambler extra-value features at no extra cost, like Weather Eye Heating, Deep-Dip rustproofing, Ceramic-Armored exhaust system. Try it—just for sport!
American Motors—Dedicated to Excellence

Free! 1965 Automotive X-Ray Book At Your Rambler Dealer

This 48-page, full-color book makes factual side-by-side comparisons of all leading 1965 cars. Checks engines, transmissions, size, room and many other features. Hundreds of photographs and easy-to-read text give you the important information you should have before you buy any new car. Get your *free* copy of the 1965 Automotive X-Ray Book from your Rambler dealer today.

RAMBLER '65
3 SENSIBLE SPECTACULARS

Ambassador—Largest and Finest of the New Ramblers
Classic—New Intermediate-Size Rambler
American—The Compact Economy King

Marlin by Rambler

The swinging new man-size sports-fastback

New fastback excitement *Marlin* by Rambler

SPECIFICATIONS

Wheelbase 112″. Length 195″. Loaded height 54.2″. Width 74.5″. Front tread 58.6″, rear tread 57.6″. Loaded ground clearance 6″. Hypoid-gear differential. Choice of rear-axle ratios with certain engine-trans. combinations. Coil springs on all four wheels. Direct-action, independent front suspension, with sway bar on V-8's. Torque-Tube drive. Front Disc Brake diameter 11.2″. Rear flanged-drum brake diameter 10″. Power brakes. Double-Safety Brake System. Step-on parking brake. Tire size 7.35 x 14, (7.75 x 14 optional for V-8's). Fuel-tank capacity, 19 gallons. 35-amp. electronic alternator and transistorized voltage regulator are standard, 40 amp., standard with air conditioning.

STANDARD EQUIPMENT

Front Disc Brakes. Power Brakes. Wheel discs. Chrome trim moldings. Double-Safety Brake System. Self-adjusting brakes. Weather Eye Heater. Fresh-air ventilation. Engine-oil filter. Fuel filters in tank and fuel pump. Windshield-wiper power-booster fuel pump. Anti-smog engine-vent system (regular type). Cellulose-fiber carburetor air cleaner. Automatic choke. Turn signals. Heavy-duty lights. Front door armrests. Rear panel armrests. Padded instrument panel. Electric clock. Solex glass rear window (even-tint). Dual sun visors. Cigarette lighter. Two front ashtrays. Two rear ashtrays. Trunk floor covering. Floor carpeting. Individually-adjustable reclining seats. Front- and rear-seat foam cushion. Coil-spring seat construction. Rear-seat courtesy light. Non-retractable front-seat belts. Glove-box lock. Two coat hooks. Five tubeless blackwall tires, low-profile type. Ceramic-Armored muffler, tailpipe and exhaust pipe. Powr-Guard "24" Intercell Battery (50 amp. on Sixes; 60 amp., standard on V-8's, and on Sixes with air conditioning; 70 amp., optional). Hood insulation.

OPTIONAL EQUIPMENT

All-vinyl upholstery for standard individually-adjustable reclining seats. Reclining Bucket Seats (fabric or all-vinyl) with center console (or center cushion), plus front- and rear-seat fold-down armrests. Headrests (left and/or right). AM or AM/FM all-transistor radios. Duo-Coustic or Vibra-Tone rear-seat speakers. All-Season Air Conditioning. Power steering. Adjust-O-Tilt steering wheel. Power-lift windows. Twin-Grip differential. Electric windshield wipers. Whitewall tires. 7.75 x 14 tires for V-8's. Solex Glass, all or windshield only (Sunshade Solex for front and rear). Powr-Saver V-8 engine fan. Wheel discs with spinners. Wire-wheel covers with spinners. Padded sun visors. Light Group; trunk light, glove-box light, courtesy lights, parking-brake warning light and backup lights (also single option). Visibility Group "A": windshield washer, left outside mirror, inside tilt mirror and visor vanity mirror (all available separately). Visibility Group "B" same as "A", except for remote-control left outside mirror. Retractable front-seat belts, non-retractable rear-seat belts. Dowgard Full-Fill Coolant. 40-Amp alternator (standard with air conditioning). 70-Amp battery. Heavy-duty cooling system (includes H.D. radiator, H.D. fan and fan shroud, standard with air conditioning). Heavy-duty shock absorbers. Heavy-duty springs, shock absorbers. Bumper guards. Undercoating.

EXTERIOR COLORS

New long-wearing, triple-coated Lustre-Gard Acrylic Enamel. Select from 26 optional two-tones, plus Silver or Black for teardrop side-window insert. 7 solid colors that are standard: Classic Black, Antigua Red, Seaside Aqua, Frost White. Metallic colors: Marina Aqua, Atlantis Aqua, Marlin Silver.

Every 1965 Rambler carries a new-car warranty for a period of 24 months or 24,000 miles, whichever occurs first.

MARLIN PERFORMANCE SELECTOR . . . Precision-engineered power teams

ENGINE SPECIFICATIONS					TRANSMISSION & REAR AXLE RATIO AVAILABILITY				
					COLUMN-SHIFT TRANSMISSIONS			FLOOR-SHIFT (with optional bucket seats & console)	
ENGINE TYPE	DISPLACEMENT BORE & STROKE	HORSEPOWER TORQUE	COMP. RATIO FUEL	CARBURETOR	Manual 3-Speed Std.	Overdrive*	Flash-O-Matic* 3-Speed	Twin-Stick* (Overdrive)	Shift-Command* Flash-O-Matic
Standard 232 Six	232 Cubic Inches 3¾″ x 3½″	155 @ 4400 222 @ 1600	8.5:1 Regular	2-Barrel Carter	3.15:1	3.54:1	3.15:1	3.54:1	3.15:1
287 V-8*	287 Cubic Inches 3¾″ x 3¼″	198 @ 4700 280 @ 2600	8.7:1 Regular	2-Barrel Holley	3.54:1	3.54:1	2.87:1 3.15:1†	3.54:1	3.15:1 2.87:1†
327 V-8*	327 Cubic Inches 4″ x 3¼″	270 @ 4700 360 @ 2600	9.7:1 Premium	4-Barrel Holley	3.54:1	3.54:1	3.15:1 2.87:1†	3.54:1	3.15:1 2.87:1†

*Optional at extra cost.
†Optional at no extra cost.

Accessories and power features, illustrated or described in this catalog, are optional at extra cost unless otherwise specified. American Motors, whose policy is one of continuous improvement, reserves the right to discontinue or change specifications, models or prices at any time without incurring obligation.

AMERICAN MOTORS—DEDICATED TO EXCELLENCE • MARLIN • AMBASSADOR • CLASSIC • AMERICAN

Meet the Rogue.

New razzle-dazzle Rambler (yes, Rambler!) outperforms every other car in its class. (Big new engine! More standard horsepower than Corvair! Valiant! Falcon! And you too, Mustang!)

"Do Rogues really come with rally stripes?"

"No, but with the new engine they drive that way."

'66 Rambler American Rogue

TV Premiere! See the new American Motors '66 cars on "The Andy Griffith-Don Knotts-Jim Nabors Special," CBS-TV, Thursday, Oct. 7th

Read the 9 reasons why the scrappy new Rogue outclasses, outperforms, out-everythings every competing car in its fighting weight and size for 1966. 1. Newest standard Six. 199 cubes of power, torque, and thrust. (128 horses—when you need 'em! Even GM, Chrysler, and Ford don't match that!) Economy? Who else but Rambler American wins best mileage in the Mobil Economy Run year after year? **2.** Shift-Command Transmission.* Right on the floor: Two ways to handle all that power: (a) shift gears yourself or (b) set it on automatic. **3.** Reclining bucket seats. The sportiest car deserves the sportiest seats. Try and find them in Rogue's competitors'. **4.** Beautiful interiors. Sleek new vinyls and fabrics. Built-in quality that really *shows!* **5.** Double-Safety brake system. We're the only U.S. car maker—except Cadillac—that makes this vital safety feature standard equipment. (Of course, you get the industry-wide "safety package." It's standard, too.) **6.** Deep-dip rustproofing. We don't just spray it on. We dunk our cars in it—clear up to the roof. **7-8-9.** More built-in quality like extruded-aluminum grilles, all-electronic alternator, ceramic-armored exhaust system. **You've got a date with a Rogue, Oct. 7th, at your friendly Giant-Killer...your American Motors/Rambler Dealer.** *optional*

American Motors...where quality is built in, not added on.

Marlin '66. Foxiest fastback at the Auto Show!

(Even with "buckets" this fastback seats six. How? Read below.)

Bucket seats* that sit 3 in front? Simple: our special sub-cushion between the buckets. For a 2+2, pull down front and rear armrests. (Let's see any other fastback do that!) **Fastback power!** If you ever need it, our 327-cu.-in. V-8* takes you from zero to 60 in 10 seconds flat. **4-on-the-floor.*** Super-sporty transmission for the husband with

the adventurous wife. Or, Shift-Command transmission*—stick shift for him, automatic for her. **Vinyl top and deck.*** Can a Marlin look even more exclusive? Try this finishing touch. **Power disc brakes.*** Fast stops—even in the rain. **Double-Safety brake system.** Only one other U.S. passenger car

makes this standard—Cadillac. **Big-dial tachs*** and instruments? We got 'em—along with swingy interiors that feature sporty vinyls, fabrics and thick door-to-door carpeting. See the '66 Marlin at the Auto Show. Then, drive one at your friendly authorized Giant-Killer . . . your American Motors/Rambler dealer.

American Motors . . . where quality is built in, not added on.

*Optional.

AMBASSADOR • MARLIN • RAMBLER CLASSIC • RAMBLER AMERICAN

THE NOW CARS

MARLIN

Now—full-size luxury comes to the sports fast-back! Even the wind whistles at this one! Marlin: the original sports fastback—now over 201" of sleek, trim beauty on a 118" wheelbase. Now over 78" wide (wide enough for six sports, without giving each other the shoulder). Now over 18 cubic feet of trunk capacity for sports gear!

More engines. Choice of two Sixes that go like eights or four Typhoon V-8s that weren't here a year ago. Try an optional, three-speed automatic, or put 4-on-the-floor and take things into your own hands! Feel Marlin's 4-link rear suspension and wide stance take the bends out of country lanes.

Luxury appointments. Plush, coil-spring seats wherever you sit. Cushioned, acoustical ceiling wherever you look. Deep, thick pile carpeting wherever there's floor. Quality built in—so the value stays in.

Sports options. Power disc brakes, electric tachometer, deep bucket seats, sports steering wheel, special handling package, and more. (Want rally signal lights? They're standard!)

Marlin safety. Standard equipment includes: energy-absorbing steering column and deep-dish wheel; Double-Safety brakes; warning signal light to monitor both brake line systems; seat belts

(retractable in front); shoulder belt anchor plates; day/nite anti-glare mirror on double-safety pivot; and more built-in safety features to help you drive with care and confidence . . . all built into a solid, single-unit body. See Marlin today at your Now Car showroom, your **American Motors/Rambler Dealer.** He's got the only sports fastback with full-size luxury. See him—now. **THE 1967 AMERICAN MOTORS**

AMBASSADOR • MARLIN • REBEL • RAMBLER AMERICAN

How does a guy get the most out of a Marlin?

Slip a "327" V-8 under the hood, put "four" on the floor and ask your wife to stop calling it a family car.

Actually, no matter which engine you pick, your spouse will be in for a surprise: her practical "family car" will have punch that won't quit.

Marlin's two Torque Command Sixes deliver 145 and 155 hp. The three big V-8's range from 198 to 270 hp (including a new 250-hp V-8). When you stick that kind of power in a car that goes 195 inches overall, you've got a thoroughly impatient machine on your hands.

By the way. Be sure to tell your practical mate how all but the big job thrive on regular gas. She'll like your attitude.

Transmissions? You've got a tough decision to make. Standard 3-on-the-tree? Overdrive? Fully synchronized 4-speed? Or, let's say you settle on our console-mounted automatic. You get to shift . . . your wife doesn't have to. Our his and hers transmission.

Suppose you've got more ideas for fitting out your Marlin. No problem. You can get an electric tach. Power disc brakes, if you like. Power steering. Power windows. A seven-position adjustable steering wheel. And that barely scratches the surface.

What else could you want in a sports fastback?

Quality, sure. The kind a man can appreciate. Built in . . . straight from the factory.

Two separate hydraulic brake systems, for example. If one goes on the fritz there's another to stop you. Six-cylinder engines that have a completely counter-balanced crankshaft with seven main bearings. Smoothest running Sixes on the market. An exhaust system that's ceramic-coated (longest-lasting system on any American car).

You also get a body that's dipped in rustproofing right up to the roof. A power train that's sealed in a tube to protect all moving parts (an industry exclusive). A suspension system with deep-coil springs at all four wheels and a sway-bar up front.

You even get a revolutionary self-adjusting clutch on Marlin Sixes. The industry's first major clutch change in over 30 years.

So there's plenty a guy can add to get the most out of Marlin. Except quality. That we build right in.

REBEL

Rebel 550 Sports Sedan: more excitement machine for your money!

Now — the first excitement machines in the intermediate-class storm ahead — with styling, size, performance, and innovations that are leaving other intermediates way behind! Look quick at the Rebel 550 2-door Sports Sedan above and you'd swear it's an SST hardtop. Look at its price sticker and you'll see it's the lowest-priced Rebel in the line! And when you peel off the sticker, who'll know? Up front, you can order Typhoon V-8 thunder, available at 290 and 343 cubic inches. And, if you're so inclined, you can team up either one of those mighty V-8s with a butter-smooth 4-on-the-floor stick shift.

Down below, there's a newly developed wide stance that tracks like a train, and a 4-link rear suspension to gentle rough roads. Out back, there are rear side-wink lights that glow in the dark. Inside, there's more people-room than any other car in its class. And it's all mounted on a nimble 114" wheelbase.

Safety in the excitement machines. Every 1967 Rebel includes the long-awaited energy-absorbing steering column as standard equipment. In addition, there's the three-spoke deep-dish wheel; Double Safety braking system with warning signal light; 4-way flashers, seat belts front and rear (retracta-

ble in front), and more built-in safety features to help you drive with care and confidence . . . all built into a solid, single-unit body. Choose from Rebel SST hardtop or convertible; 770 hardtop, sedan or wagon; 550 sedans or wagon. There's an excitement machine that's right for your money at your American Motors/Rambler Dealer.

THE NOW CARS FROM THE 1967 AMERICAN MOTORS
AMBASSADOR · MARLIN · REBEL · RAMBLER AMERICAN

READ HOW YOUR INVESTMENT IS PROTECTED BY THIS GREAT NEW WARRANTY: [warranty fine print]

QUALITY BUILT IN — SO THE VALUE STAYS IN.

"There isn't a better intermediate size car sold in the United States than the 1967 Rebel"
says Tom McCahill, automobile expert for Mechanix Illustrated.

"Frankly, I never thought I'd be making such a statement."

Tom McCahill evaluates the automobile industry for Mechanix Illustrated. Recently, he took out an SST hardtop equipped with a 343 cu. in. Typhoon V-8. How did our Excitement Machine perform?

"In roadability and performance, it would top most of the newer specialty cars. There's absolutely no plowing and little body roll. The whole feel of the car, when going over ruts or across dirt roads, is excellent."

What about comfort? "In straight-line driving the SST is as comfortable as the Jell-O specials."

How about Rebel's new four-link rear suspension?

"Of all the new sporty-type cars, as they come from the showroom, Rebel has by far the best and safest suspension of the whole kit and caboodle."

And the looks? "As sharp in appearance as a thousand-dollar bill. And from a cost angle, Rebel's not overpriced."

This is your kind of car, created for '67 by American Motors. A six-passenger Excitement Machine that gives you more excitement for the money.

See your American Motors/Rambler Dealer. Then do what Tom did. Take a test-drive.

American Motors builds your kind of car
AMBASSADOR · MARLIN · REBEL · RAMBLER AMERICAN

AMERICAN MOTORS

The new AMX will be sold as democratically as possible.

We, American Motors, have over 2,300 dealers across the country who can sell more AMX's than we can make.

And we will only make about 10,000 this year.

In other words, we're faced with a mini-Supply of AMX's and a maxi-Demand for AMX's.

In an effort to give everyone an equal chance to buy an AMX, we're resorting to the best solution we can think of.

Like the House of Representatives, we will try to send a fair share of AMX's to each state, based on its proportionate population.

For example, California, with a larger share of the people, should receive a larger share of AMX's.

New Hampshire, with fewer people, won't get quite so many.

It should all work out democratically.

What Is It?

The AMX is a 2-seater. For people who love sports cars, but haven't the time or the money to take care of one.

Priced at under $3,300, the AMX offers most of the advantages of a high-priced foreign car.

With none of the disadvantages associated with owning a high performance sports car.

The costly disadvantages of constant maintenance and special engine tune-ups.

In short, the AMX gives you the ease of maintenance associated with a family sedan, along with the sheer fun and maneuverability of a sports car costing thousands more.

The Engine. One Size Fits All.

The AMX body is made of steel. Which, while strong, is also heavy.

So we tried an imaginative technique for reducing the AMX's total weight.

We selected a lightweight engine block that combusts exactly the same power as a heavy block.

It worked.

The AMX engine cradle will hold any of three different engines:

Our 290 cubic inch.

Our 343 cubic inch.

Our 390 cubic inch. (Zero to 60 in under 7 seconds. One, two, three, four, five, six, sev—that fast.)

The incredibly *uncomplex* design of the AMX means that, once the 390's broken in, you could roll right onto a race track and be ready to do about 130 mph.

In pure stock form—without special engine modifications.

All three engines are V-8 configuration, and use similar engine blocks.

Which means you don't add excessive size and weight as you go from the 290 to the 343 to the 390.

And though there are cars on the road that are faster than the AMX, we hasten to add that beating other drivers isn't the AMX's main appeal.

Handling.

In the auto industry "handling" means how fast and how accurately your car responds to your personal driving technique.

And how easily.

It's the way the car reacts to you *as you drive*, not the usual dull split second later. You get out of the lane, pass the car in front and get back into lane in one sure motion.

The AMX offers one of the fastest steering wheel ratios of any U.S.-built car.

This means it turns, corners, follows your direction *simultaneously*.

You. The Layman.

If car advertising never tells you about engineering, it's only because you'd never understand.

Ahhhh...but then again, maybe you would.

AMX standard equipment includes a 290 cubic inch V-8 with 4-barrel carburetor, rated at 225 HP, a short throw, all-syncromesh 4-on-the-floor, dual exhausts, fiberglass belted wide-profile tires, slim-shelled reclining bucket seats, 8,000 RPM tach, padded aircraft-type instrument panel with deep-set controls, energy absorbing steering column, heavy duty springs and shocks, large diameter sway bar, rear traction bars.

And more.

Are Two Seats Enough?

Yes.

There are 78,000,000 cars in this country with enough seating capacity to carry 450,000,000 people.

Or one-seventh the population of the entire world.

However, there are only 200,000,000 people in America.

Leaving 250,000,000 more car seats than people to sit in them.

Ask yourself if you really need more than a 2-seater. Your answer may surprise you.

AMX Inner Space.

While the AMX isn't much of a place to hold meetings, it will hold a lot of sport things because it is a sports car.

Back of the dual bucket seats is a fully-carpeted floor space.

It's not as big as a trunk, but we can verify that it will hold any of the following: 3 good-sized suitcases, a big TV set, 2 scuba-diving outfits, 4 parachutes, 3 electric guitars and amplifiers.

Things of that nature.

Or, you can leave it empty.

And keep the space a space.

AMX Inner Space Part II.

If you need more space, the AMX trunk is where you'll find it.

It's a lot bigger than you'd expect a sports car trunk to be.

This is possible because we didn't fill the trunk with a big spare tire.

We gave you The Airless Spare.

When you need it, it "wwwwhhhhooooosshh!" inflates.

The Airless Spare is something every car should have.

Because it doesn't take up trunk space with air that you don't need.

AMX Outer Space.

You might think that a car offering all of the luggage space of the AMX must be a pretty long car.

But the AMX is an amazing *five inches* shorter than the Corvette.

And the Corvette is pretty short.

Will AMX Number 14 Be More Valuable Than AMX Number 777?

When you buy your AMX, its production number will be set in the dash.

While this may mean a lot to collectors in the years ahead, we do want to point out that all AMX's are made with the same attention and quality.

And while possessing a lower number may have a sentimental or prestige value, it does not in any way make one AMX better than another.

Test Drive.

Before you rush out to buy the new AMX, you should know where to rush to.

The good old phone book has a listing for the American Motors dealer nearest you.

He'll arrange your test drive of the new AMX.

If he still has one.

American Motors

Ambassador · Rebel · Rambler American · Javelin · And the new AMX

American Motors Sales Corp.
Box 50-A
Detroit, Michigan 48232   Dept. L

Dear Sirs:

As a legal resident of the Sovereign State of _____ I would like to test drive the AMX before there are no AMX's left to buy. While I am looking up the name of the American Motors dealer nearest me, please send me a copy of the AMX Story.

Name _____

Address _____

City _____ Zip _____

1. Based upon manufacturer's suggested retail price, federal taxes included. State and local taxes, destination charges, options, excluded.

have REBEL–am traveling!

Four-time national drag champion Hayden Proffitt.

As in 1967, the 1968 Grant REBEL SST is a flip top.

That's champion driver Hayden Proffitt behind the wheel of the powerful *NEW* 1968 Grant REBEL SST funny car! And he's traveling—traveling the quarter-mile in 38 cities of the U.S. and Canada!

Hayden believes the new Grant REBEL SST will run up an even greater score than the 1967 Rebel which broke the national speed record for ⅛ mile tracks and set six new ¼ mile track records! Hayden says it's the greatest car he's ever driven!

The 1968 Grant REBEL SST is powered by American Motors' new V-8 engine, which Grant enlarged to 438 cubic inches and modified to include fuel injection and a supercharger! At 9,000 rpm, it produces 1,200 horsepower!

Before each race date, the new Grant REBEL SST will be displayed in an American Motors / Rambler dealership!

Watch for it. Watch it go!

Grant INDUSTRIES
3680 Beverly Boulevard
Los Angeles, California 90004

/ **AMERICAN MOTORS**
14250 Plymouth Road
Detroit, Michigan 48232

Running a Champion-equipped modified 290 CID AMX 24 hours straight—a team of drivers headed by Craig Breedlove and sanctioned by USAC sweeps 90 FIA Class C closed car speed records at an average 140.790 mph! In Class B, the same team set 16 new marks in a 390 CID AMX—again on Champions!

American Motors' all-new AMX shatters 106 national and international speed records—sparked by <u>Champions</u>! Here's more proof Champion spark plugs deliver <u>outstanding</u> performance. Add Champion's record-setting spark to your car—today!

Champion spark plugs ...the heart of a tune-up!

DEPENDABLE
CHAMPION
SPARK PLUGS

CHAMPION SPARK PLUG COMPANY · TOLEDO, OHIO 43601

HOT ROD: JUNE '68. AMERICAN MOTORS WAS REALLY ON THE WAR-PATH BY ENDORSING THE GRANT INDUSTRIES REBELS.

HOT ROD: JULY '68

American Motors Modified.

Since we discovered racing, we just haven't been the same. We know one thing. This is no mere infatuation. It's love.

Our intentions are serious, and we can prove it:

Javelin

Two of our Javelins have been specially prepared to compete in Trans-Am road racing events. As of this writing we've been in three of them.

At Sebring we were fifth. At Lime Rock we took a third. And at Warbonnet, Oklahoma we came in second and fourth. Then at Mid-Ohio we led the trials with both the first and second fastest qualifiers and broke the track sedan lap record.

We're also sponsoring the building and campaigning of a new Javelin "Funny Car" under the supervision of Doug Thorley, one of the famous names in drag racing.

There is a NASCAR Javelin, too, on the "GT" circuit under private sponsorship.

For one so young, Javelin's been around.

AMX

Even before we officially introduced the AMX, it broke 90 Class C records (with a modification of the standard 290 CID engine bored out to 304 CID). AMX's average speed for 24 hours was 140.790 MPH.

And 16 Class B records (with a modification of the optional 390 CID engine bored out to 397 CID).

Craig and Lee Breedlove were the drivers. Every FIA record they set was sanctioned by USAC.

Rebel

A new Rebel "Funny Car" has been built (under our sponsorship) by Grant Industries of Los Angeles.

This association was very successful last year, setting new ¼ mile track records of 8.11 seconds and 180.85 MPH at Tampa.

At the end of last season Hayden Proffitt had established six track records and one national speed record with the Rebel.

Not bad for a first season.

Rambler American

A Rambler American 2-Door Sedan won first place in a SCCA National Sports Car Race on June 9th at Huntsville, Alabama in the over-two-liter sedan class.

This was the second consecutive victory for this privately owned Rambler American. Not bad for an economy car.

Navarro/Rambler "Indy Car"

We're backing a program to further develop the Rambler six-powered Navarro Injection Special, a championship Indy race car.

The 199 CID six (standard in the Rambler American) equipped with a turbo-supercharger, toured the Indy track at 153 MPH during the 1967 qualification week. The fastest any six ever did there.

This year the car is much faster with fuel injection. But unfortunately it suffered a mild crash in practice runs.

Maybe a six taking on the big boys at Indy was over-ambitious. Maybe not.

As of yet, we don't know our own strength.

A sports car for the price of a sporty car.

The 1970 AMX is the only American sports car that costs less than $4,000.

It lists for $3,395, which puts it into the same price category as a loaded Mustang or Camaro.

But there is where the similarity begins and ends.

For the AMX is a legitimate two-seater sports car. Not because we say it is, but because that's the way we built it.

Our 360 cu. in. V-8 engine isn't optional. It's standard.

You don't pay extra for contoured high-back bucket seats with integral head restraints.

Or mag style wheels.

And an all-synchromesh 4-on-the-floor with Hurst shifter, dual exhausts, fiberglass belted Polyglas™ tires, heavy duty shocks and springs, rear torque links, a 140 m.p.h. speedometer and a big tach aren't part of a long list of available options.

They're part of a long list of standard equipment.

Sure, the AMX offers a larger engine and other performance options.

But you don't need them to make the AMX a sports car.

You've got that to begin with.

◢◤ American Motors
$3,395 AMX

1. Manufacturer's suggested retail price. Federal taxes included. State and local taxes, if any, destination charges and options excluded.

St. Jovite, Quebec, August 2—American Motors' Javelin beats Mustang, Challenger and Camaro in the Le Circuit Trans Am.

Mark down Mark Donohue and Javelin as a winning combination.

They've collaborated on 3 victories out of the last 4 Trans Ams.

The most recent was consummated with ease.

Donohue finished over one minute ahead of the second place Mustang driven by George Follmer.

Parnelli Jones, in a Mustang, was third. Sam Posey, in a Challenger, was fourth.

And Peter Revson, in a Javelin, finished fifth.

In overall points Mustang leads with 56. We've got 43 and Camaro's got 30.

But we're closing in. And Watkins Glen awaits.

If you're going to buy a sporty car, buy one that's going places.

◢▮ American Motors

American Motors dealers are celebrating the fastest finish of the year with the best deals of the year.

The past three months have been exciting for us.

Mark Donohue, in the SCCA Trans-Am Series, and Jim Paschal, in NASCAR's Grand American Circuit, have been driving their specially-prepared and modified Javelins to victories all over the map.

Between them they've won 9 out of the last 13 races they entered. Such a record deserves recognition.

So, for the next two weeks we're celebrating. With special prices and special deals on every 1970 Javelin we've got. Which is only fitting.

We figure if Donohue and Paschal are going to beat Mustangs, Camaros, Firebirds, Challengers and Barracudas on the track, the least we can do is try to beat them on the deals we're offering you.

If you're going to buy a sporty car, buy one that's going places.

◢▮ American Motors

To locate your nearest American Motors dealer, call as you normally dial, long distance no charge. (800) 243-6000 any time, any day. In Connecticut, (800) 942-0655.

We made the Javelin the hairiest looking sporty car in America, even at the risk of scaring some people off.

The new Javelin may not be quite as lovable as the old Javelin, but it's a lot tougher.

We made it longer, wider and lower to make it ride better.

And to make it look better while it's riding better, we sculptured the fenders and raised them around the tires.

We sculptured the hood, too, into a fast, glacial slope.

We panelled the roof with a twin-canopy and a rear spoiler lip.

Then, of course, we had to create something for the inside, so it could keep pace with the outside.

A new "curved cockpit" instrument panel that may make you feel more like a pilot than a driver.

And if that isn't enough for you to intimidate friends and/or competitors, we're offering a range of engines up to a 401 CID 4-barrel V-8.

We may lose a few librarians for customers, but we think we'll gain a few purists.

If you had to compete with GM, Ford and Chrysler what would you do? ◢▮ American Motors

All sporty cars look pretty much the same, cost pretty much the same, and act pretty much the same.
Except the 1980 looking Javelin.

The original idea of the sporty car was to give you a car with some individuality.

But lately, all the sporty cars are looking pretty much alike.

So, at American Motors, we went all-out to make our Javelin a really different-looking car. Even at the risk of scaring some people off.

The fenders rise and fall in an aerodynamic whoosh around the tires.

The grill and hood slope to a canopy roof with a rear spoiler lip.

And on the inside, the smooth racy feeling of the outside carries through. The "cockpit" instrument panel. The high-back buckets in vinyl or optional fabric or leather.

But not only did we make the Javelin look good, we made it drive good. It's longer, lower, and wider for a smoother ride. The steering ratio is quicker and the suspension is tougher for faster, tighter cornering.

And to make the Javelin really go like it looks, we've got engines from a base 6 all the way up to an optional 401 cubic inch V8. Which are available in all the Javelin models: the Javelin; the luxurious Javelin SST; and the brawny Javelin AMX, the car Trans-Am race driver Mark Donohue helped us design.

All in all, we've achieved one very important thing with the new Javelin: Before, you were stuck with the choice of either getting a sporty car that looked like the others, or spending a lot of money for one that looked different.

Now you can get a Javelin. For a basic list price of only $2879.*

American Motors ◢▮

Jeep guts.
Never before so strong or so sporty.

Jeep Commando.
Newly designed with the most powerful engines ever and the brightest colors.

This isn't just a new model of an old favorite. This Jeep Commando is a whole new vehicle.

Take its strength. Jeep guts make this Commando the strongest one ever built. With a hefty 232 CID 6-cylinder engine as standard equipment. And a 304 CID V-8 as a mighty option. That's power. They'll take you places you never dared go before.

Take its looks. That new front end makes the Commando more stylish than ever—along with the nine bright, up-to-date colors you have to choose from. This 4-wheel drive vehicle looks at home—at home!

And take the interior. The Commando adds more of everything you want. More leg room. And more knee, hip and elbow room, too. More comfort with full-foam bench seats available in both the front and rear. (Those smart foam-molded bucket seats are still standard.) And more luxury, too, with extra trims and options.

Altogether, it's the new Jeep Commando—the most exciting new 4-wheel drive vehicle in America.

Toughest 4-letter word on wheels.
Jeep

Drive your Jeep vehicle with care and keep America the Beautiful.

THE CLOSEST YOU CAN COME TO OWNING THE TRANS-AM CHAMPION.

Last year Mark Donohue raced our specially prepared Javelin-AMX to seven victories over Mustang and Camaro and clinched our first SCCA Trans-Am championship.

So with a track record like this, you'd expect to get a great sporty car when you buy the Javelin-AMX. But you also get something you wouldn't expect.

You get a car that's been checked over so thoroughly that we make this promise: If anything goes wrong and

it's our fault, we'll fix it free. And if we have to keep your car overnight to fix it, over 1900 dealers will loan you a car. Free. Finally, you get a name and toll free number to call in Detroit if you have a problem.

The 1972 Javelin-AMX and American Motors Buyer Protection Plan. You won't get a car like this or a plan like this from anyone else.

AMERICAN MOTORS

MOTOR TREND: JANUARY '72. MOST WOULD NOT CONSIDER JEEPS AS TRUE MUSCLE CARS, BUT WITH 302 CUBIC INCHES, THEY INDEED HAD "GUTS."

CAR CRAFT: FEBRUARY '72

THE ONLY SPORTY CAR
YOU CAN GET WITH A 360 V-8
WITHOUT GETTING IN OVER YOUR HEAD.

For about $2700* you can get the Hornet X with rally stripes, slot-style wheels, fat tires, a sports steering wheel, and optional 360 CID V-8 automatic. If you wanted an engine this big and equipment like this on any other car, you'd have to go to more than $3100.

You also get something with the Hornet X you can't get anywhere else at any price. The American Motors Buyer Protection Plan.

What it promises is that if anything goes wrong with the car, and it's our fault, we'll fix it free. And if we have to keep your car overnight to fix it, over 1900 dealers will loan you a car Free. Finally, you get a name and toll-free number to call in Detroit if you have a problem.

With a car and a Plan like this, why buy a sporty car from anyone else? You don't be getting in over your head.

AMERICAN MOTORS

A GREMLIN WITH THE HEART OF A JAVELIN.
THE GREMLIN X WITH A 304 V-8.

You are looking at the most powerful small car made in America. The Gremlin X with our optional 304 V-8 engine, the same engine that comes standard on our Javelin-AMX.

Other sporty subcompacts give you the impression of being zippy and tough, too. But no amount of fat stripes or hood scoops can hide the fact that the largest engine you'll get on any of them is 4 cylinders with a maximum of 140 CID.

To go with its V-8 engine, the Gremlin X also comes with a wide range of performance equipment.

Fat Polyglas® tires. A beefy rear axle. Wide rim sport wheels. Big brakes. Rear torque links.

Full-synchro floor-shift. Front sway bar. Special shocks and springs. A sports steering wheel. And 2 contoured bucket seats that won't help you go faster, but will make you more comfortable.

This year, the '72 Gremlin X also comes with something you wouldn't expect on a sporty small car. The American Motors Buyer Protection Plan.

It's a program that takes care of you after you buy the car. And nobody in the business has anything like it.

No matter why you buy the Gremlin X, though, your biggest joy in owning it will come on the day you can take it out for a drive and play King of the Road.

¹Optional

American Motors

We Won!
Now you win with the
Trans Am* Victory Javelin

For the second year in a row, specially prepared and modified Javelins beat all the other hot cars in the Trans American Racing Series and we feel like celebrating.

We won the championship, and now with the specially equipped Trans Am Victory Javelin, you get 14" slot style wheels, E-70 x 14 white lettered wide polyglas tires, space-saver spare tire and a Trans Am winner medallion on the side panel at no extra charge.

We call it the Trans Am Victory Package American Motors includes this special

equipment listing for $167.45 at no cost.

And remember, only American Motors makes this promise: The Buyer Protection Plan backs every '73 car we build and we'll see that our dealers back that promise.

So come see the winner at your American Motors dealer and find out why we say: We back them better because we build them better.

George Follmer,
Roy Woods:
Trans-Am Racing Team

Manufacturer's suggested retail price of the
specially equipped Trans Am Victory Javelin is
$2959.00. State and local taxes not included, destination
charges and other options extra.
*SCCA Inc. is the proprietor of the marks "Trans-Am" and "SCCA"

Buckle up for safety.

AMC ◢▮ Javelin
We back them better because we build them better.

Chapter Two

Chrysler Corporation

Chrysler Division

RARE TREAT It is a simple matter of fact that Chrysler's famed 300 models have never taken kindly to mass production. ¶ The 300-H, newest member of this spicy clan, is no exception. A close look at its impeccable grooming discloses the reasons why. ¶ Individual bucket seats provide carefully fitted leather comfort for four and a full complement of gauges and controls include a tachometer. Steering is power-assisted, as are the brakes. Handling is superb. This is the car that first brought the designation Grand Touring back to the American automobile. ¶ The 300-H is a car that delights in the 600-mile day. Urge it to greater effort and a lusty 380 horsepower V-8 flames into action. The H can slice through traffic with an ease that belies its stature. And then proceed to obliterate the miles with a confidence no domestic rival can duplicate. ¶ Obviously, Chrysler doesn't pour this one into a mold and rush it down the line. And wouldn't try to if it could.

CHRYSLER 300-H A rare kind of car for a rare kind of man.

MOTOR TREND: JANUARY '62. RARE IS THE PERFECT WORD FOR THIS 300 "H" AS ONLY ABOUT 120 CONVERTIBLES WERE BUILT.

300 (1955) *Grandsire of a great line of sports-bred Chryslers. First production automobile with 300-horsepower rating. Proved in the Pan American Road Race.*

300-B (1956) *First place champion of the demanding Daytona High Performance Trials. NASCAR and AAA title-holder. Took to the dirt tracks as readily as the road.*

300-C (1957) *Acclaimed by international design experts as the "perfect example of modern architecture." Scored big repeat performance as Daytona champion.*

300-D (1958) *Specially designed suspension system gets the nod from the magazine experts. Car testers call this one a "great handler in every driving situation."*

300-E (1959) *This one outperformed its illustrious predecessors—streaking from a standing start to 60 mph in 8.4 spine-tingling seconds!*

300-F (1960) *Captured first 6 places in the Daytona High Performance Trials. Clinched its title as undisputed champion of hardtops in this "all-out" contest.*

300-G (1961) *Rare road artist and rally car! Again won orchids from the auto experts on performance and handling. Won flying mile "Beach Run" again at Daytona Beach.*

300-H (1962) *Aptly titled "The Beautiful Brute" in a three-part article running in Car and Driver. This exciting story of its heritage and talents was later published in book form.*

And now... **CHRYSLER 300-J**

the ninth and newest of Chrysler's hot-blooded clan

True to the tradition of its thoroughbred background . . . and by every performance standard, the 300-J is ready to stake its claim as the first great name in America's Grand Touring automobiles.

Its walloping ramjet engine proved its punch in a test run at the Indianapolis Speedway. Here the "J" streaked from a standing start to 60 mph in *7 sizzling seconds!* Yet, so sure are Chrysler dealers of the basic strength of the "J's" magnificent V-8 engine (and the major parts that carry power to the rear wheels), they warrant* it for 5 years or 50,000 miles of the hardest driving possible.

The "J's" race-bred torsion-bar suspension provides track-sure handling. Its precision steering has few equals in the world of sports-bred automobiles. Comfort comes in contoured bucket seats that adjust individually for front seat passengers.

300-J. Born and bred for driving. Built in limited numbers. Perhaps you may be among the fortunate few to own it.

Your authorized Chrysler Dealer's Warranty against defects in material and workmanship on 1963 cars has been expanded to include parts replacement or repair, without charge for required parts or labor, for 5 years or 50,000 miles, whichever comes first, on the engine block, head and internal parts; transmission case and internal parts (excluding manual clutch); torque converter, drive shaft, universal joints (excluding dust covers), rear axle and differential, and rear wheel bearings, provided the vehicle has been serviced at reasonable intervals according to the Chrysler Certified Car Care schedules.

CHRYSLER DIVISION **CHRYSLER** MOTORS CORPORATION

MOTOR TREND: MARCH '63. THE ENTIRE 300 LETTER SERIES, UP TO 1963, IS BEAUTIFULLY PRESENTED IN THIS SINGLE AD.

300·K Chrysler's fiery-spirited full-size sports car. Its performance heritage goes ten years deep. Its predecessors in Chrysler's famed letter series were the equal of Gran Tourismo automobiles the world over. This one, too, is an exceptional road machine. The "K" is powered by Chrysler's husky 413 cu.-in. V-8, now modified to move out even faster in passing gear. You can choose a ram-inducted, twin 4-barrel version* that's hairy-chested enough to match your wildest dreams. Comes in Convertible and 2-Door Hardtop models, with such American-style comforts as power steering, power brakes and automatic transmission standard.

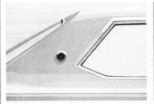  

Left to right above: Colorful 300-K medallion, on C-pillar of 2-Door Hardtop, on front fenders of Convertible. New floor-mounted 4-speed manual transmission* is available with standard 300-K engine. Standard between-seat console adds sport-style luxury. It features a Performance Indicator, lockable compartment and automatic transmission shift lever with lighted quadrant. *Optional at extra cost.

300-K STANDARD EQUIPMENT ■ TorqueFlite automatic transmission ■ Power steering ■ Power brakes ■ Between-seat console with a Performance Indicator ■ FirePower 360 V-8 with 4-barrel carburetor ■ Dual exhausts ■ Electric clock ■ Deluxe steering wheel ■ Back-up lights ■ Glove and luggage compartment lights ■ Windshield washers.

300-K Convertible in Formal Black with tan interior.

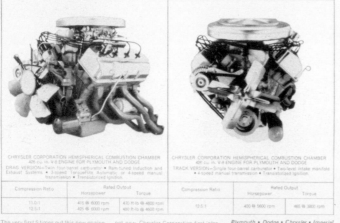
Dodge Division

DART 440 "GREAT POWER-TO-WEIGHT!"

Champion dragster Don Garlits had just popped Dart 440 from zero to sixty in 8.1 seconds; he had also traveled the quarter mile from a standing start in 15.4 seconds. "That's quite a bomb," he observed enthusiastically after his informal test runs. "The boys are going to win some trophies with this machine. It's got a very good power-to-weight ratio."

His Dart 440 was equipped strictly for street use. Standard 3.23 axle, 3-speed automatic transmission and 361 cu. in. V8. Dart 440 does have a great power-to-weight ratio. It's as high as one horse for every eleven pounds.

"As far as I've ever known, acceleration is simply a matter of power to weight," observed West Coast dragster Jack Chrisman, who along with Garlits was one of nine auto experts we asked to Detroit last summer to test our new Dart 440. We had done some interesting and original things with this new car. Size was one.

We eliminated excess overhang and useless sheet metal to make the car more maneuverable, more parkable, easier to steer. In doing so, of course, we eliminated dead weight. And Zoom! That's what you get when you pack a standard 318 cu. in. V8 into the new size Dodge Dart. Pack a 318 with power-pack, or the husky 361 cu. in. job, and, mister, you do have a bomb.

"This is a drag racer you can drive on the streets," added Chrisman. "It's smooth and quiet. It looks like a race car and handles like one. The cornering is good and so is the straight-away handling. It's the kind of car I'd want."

Sportswriter Max Muhleman, of the Charlotte News, put it this way: "You could win a trophy in a quarter mile and then drive home a crate of eggs without worrying about breaking them."

We'd like to add just one point. That good power-to-weight works both ways. You get action . . . and we're pretty sure you'll like the good gas savings. It's part of the bonus that goes with the new size Dodge Dart.

We think this is an enthusiast's kind of car. We'd like you to try it and judge for yourself. Okey? Go see your dependable Dodge Dealer.

SIZED RIGHT IN THE MIDDLE OF THE BIG AND LITTLE—DODGE DART

HOT ROD: JUNE '62. WHAT AN IMPOSING IMAGE THIS STAGGERED-DESIGN TWO FOUR-BARREL MONSTER PRESENTED IN ITS DAY . . . IT STILL DOES!

INTRODUCING THE FANTASTIC POLARA 500. You have never driven an automobile like this one. It is definitely not for the casual driver. This limited-production 1962 Dodge is powered by a lusty 361 cubic inch V8, with four-barrel carburetion, a high-performance cam, and dual exhausts. The interior is magnificent. Saddle-grained vinyl upholstery. Individually adjustable bucket seats. Courtesy console. Sill-to-sill carpeting. Available as a convertible (shown) or in a hard-top series. One more point. The 1962 Dodge Polara 500 is a very special automobile. Don't expect everybody to own one. *COME IN AND DRIVE THE NEW LEAN BREED OF DODGE.*

THE DEPENDABLES ARE HERE !

IF YOU'RE LOOKING FOR THUNDER

THIS IS WHERE THE LIGHTNING STRIKES

HOT 1963 DODGE

You've found what you're looking for: The bucket-seat Dodge that takes a back seat to nobody. The Polara 500! No mere piece of transportation, this one. Put your foot down and 383 cubes sock you off the line with a jolt. This two-barrel brand of lightning is standard in the Polara 500 (so are a console, carpeting, all-vinyl, buckets, the works). This engine is also available as an option on other 1963 Dodge models, from cinder-kickin' sedans to walloping wagons. Or you can get it with four barrels and up the action even more. If you want to tear up the strips, just say so. You can lay it on hotter'n a charcoal bed with the new 426 Ram Charger that'll burn rubber as long as you let it. In all, Dodge offers a whole stable full of hard charging V8s, starting with a standard 318 cuber. (Nothing to sneeze at either; it packs more power per pound than most any standard going.) Don't settle for less. Put your foot down soon at your dependable Dodge Dealer.

A FULL LINE OF CARS IN THE LOW-PRICE FIELD !

THE DEPENDABLES FROM DODGE !

A WOLF...

IN STREET CLOTHING

THE DEPENDABLES BUILT BY DODGE !

426 CUBES

COOL OFF ANY STRIP

Stock car racing is the ultimate measure of a car's capabilities. And the '63 Dodge has been doing very well, thank you. Fact is, it's chewing up competition on tracks all over the country. We aren't the least bit surprised. Racing takes raw power and Dodge has it. Racing takes control. Dodge has that, too. Experts call its torsion-bar suspension the best in the business. Racing demands toughness. Dodge's unitized body is welded, one piece. Tough, tight. As rattle-free as can be. What's best is this: All the things that make Dodge such a wolf on the tracks make it a model of deportment for your everyday driving. Performance? You've got it—with a wide choice of prize-winning V8 power. You've got a lot more going for you, too. Maneuverability, money-saving dependability and something extra nice—a low price. Dodge is on the move, all right. And we urge you to sample some of its high adventure soon. See your Dodge Dealer. He's got The Dependables in a size to suit you. Compact Dart. Standard-size Dodge. Big 880. Pick a size, pick a price, pick a Dodge.

HOT 1963 DODGE

DODGE DIVISION ◆ **CHRYSLER** MOTORS CORPORATION | '63 DODGE: A FULL LINE OF CARS IN THE LOW-PRICE FIELD. THREE SERIES: 24 MODELS: HARDTOPS, SEDANS, CONVERTS, WAGONS.

Lay on our 426-cube V8 and . . . ZAP! Drag records fall* like pelted partridges. That's because horsepower comes so close to matching displacement that few moving things are its equal.

The 426's stablemates, too, give you more rubber-scorching potential than competition. There's the 383 with four barrels. The 383 with two. And the 318, our standard V8, that'll out-drag, about any standard engine in the low-price field. This one's remarkably thrifty, too.

And here's one thing to remember. There are 24 models of the standard-size '63 Dodge. Every one is in the low-price field! See them at your Dodge Dealer.

HOT 63 DODGE

*Records here to fall. The 426 cube V8 replaces the 413 Ramcharger which has trusted local and sanctioned-fixed records all over the country. Here are just four national Hot Rod Association records established: AA/D JIM NELSON 8.99 ET—S5, S DICK LADDEN 13.71 ET—S5/SA "MAVERICK" 12.50 ET— A/FX GEORGE PARKINSON 12.26.

DODGE DIVISION ◆ **CHRYSLER** MOTORS CORPORATION

Jim Thornton and Herman Mozer (979) coming off the line in S/SA class.

Some days you win

Mozer and Al Eckstrand in final run for Top Stock Eliminator title.

Some days you lose

The fortunes on the straight and narrow warpath change as quickly as the gears in the go-box! Today you tear 'em up. Tomorrow is another day. Your machine has got to be mean . . . you've got to be good . . . and you've got to come out of the hole with more togetherness than Amos and Andy! That's the drama of the drag strip, man and machine.

That's why more than 100,000 buffs bulged the track at Indy for the NHRA's big showdown—the world championships.

And what a showdown! On Saturday, Jim Thornton in a '63 Dodge downed his Ramcharger teammate, Herman Mozer, on his way to royalty in the Super Stock Automatic Class. Next day, running for the meet's most coveted honor—Top Stock Eliminator—Mozer turned the tables and gave Thornton the thumb. But the event was far from over. Mozer still had to face the present "Mr. Eliminator," Al Eckstrand in Lawman, another specially equipped '63 Dodge. And another winner is defeated. Mozer edged him by 1/100th of a second with an e.t. of 12.22.

Some days you win. Some days you lose. That's what keeps the quarter-mile jaunt so interesting. But have you noticed? When a Dodge loses these days . . . it's to another Dodge.

Hot Dodge

DODGE DIVISION  CHRYSLER MOTORS CORPORATION

Rebel Rouser

Face it. There's a bit of rebel in each of us. Balking at the battle of the budget. Ready to kick the dull driving habit. Fed up on cars with tired blood. Rise up and let the rebel in you dig that tempting new beauty above. 1966 Dodge Coronet 500. Aimed right at your adrenaline glands. Its swingin' styling gift-wraps performance that runs from *pow* to *wow!* Four hot V8s—from standard 273-incher to optional 4-barrel 383-inch growler—supply the go. Inside, strictly show. Take a look at those contour-comfort bucket seats. Standard. Like deep-pile carpeting, padded dash and long center console. (Not to mention an optional new tach that swivels for easy eyeballing.) Shows you some class? Part of the plot, man. The beautiful Coronet 500 plot: to move you first-cabin at tourist rates. Investigate it. We don't think you can find a car with Coronet-type action, looks and all-round pizzaz for Coronet's price. So c'mon, reb. Join the drive on Dullsville. Drive a '66 Dodge Coronet.

'66 Dodge Coronet

DODGE DIVISION CHRYSLER MOTORS CORPORATION

MOTOR TREND: MARCH '64. ONE OF THE MOST POPULAR NAMES AT THE DRAG STRIPS WAS THE DODGE "RAMCHARGERS."

CAR LIFE: NOVEMBER '65

This is Dodge Charger

Charger, the dream car that's no dream. It's here. Right now. At your Dodge dealer's. A big, brawny, powerful fastback that's all primed up and ready to take on the best. Charger-style. And this is Charger style. retractable headlights that function automatically. Hefty V8 power. Buckets, fore and aft. Dash-mounted tach. Full length console. Rear seats that convert into a spacious cargo compartment so when the buckets go down, load space goes up. All standard equipment. With all the class and dash you knew a dream car had to have. If it ever came true. And now it has – at your Dodge dealer's. Climb into Charger. Fire up the engine. Head out on the road. In about three blocks you'll be really hooked.

Dodge Charger
DODGE DIVISION · CHRYSLER MOTORS CORPORATION

...new leader of the Dodge Rebellion.

Boss Hoss

Dodge Charger with a big, tough 426 Street Hemi up front makes other steeds look staid. Both for show and go. Charger looks beautifully quick just standing still. And the optional Hemi V8 supplies a kick to match, with 425 muscular horses. Not a pony or a kitten in the bunch. The hot setup? You bet. Consider. When you order Dodge Charger with the Street Hemi, you get heavy-duty suspension, 4-ply nylon Blue Streak tires, and big 11-inch brakes as part of the package. A balanced package engineered from the pavement up to be safer, more controllable and secure on any road. If your driving conditions are such that you want to give your Charger an even better brake, front disc binders are optional (for '66 Coronet, too). If you're looking for the combination that's really boss any way you look at it, check out Dodge Charger. Learn what it's like to be king of the road. See your nearest Dodge dealer and slide behind the wheel of this hot new leader of the Dodge Rebellion.

Dodge Charger
DODGE DIVISION · CHRYSLER MOTORS CORPORATION

Dodge Charger—named "Top Performance Car of the Year" by CARS magazine.

EVEN CUSTER COULDN'T MUSTER
A STAMPEDE LIKE THIS

Dodge Charger musters enough horses, with optional 426 Hemi V8 or 440-Magnum, to mount up a whole cavalry troop. And then some. Along with each of these smooth, powerful, responsive performers, you get a whole package of special handling equipment to make America's first full-sized fastback behave like a thoroughbred: heavy-duty suspension, high-performance nylon tires, and big 11-inch brakes (with discs optional up front). Every Charger has a dash-mounted tach, front buckets and fold-down rear seats, full-width taillights, plus disappearing head lamps that blend beautifully with the front end styling. Check it out for yourself . . . Dodge Charger, a balanced automobile engineered for the enthusiast.

It's Dodge Rebellion Operation '67

'67 Dodge Charger

DODGE DIVISION **CHRYSLER** MOTORS CORPORATION

THE SILKEN SNARL

DODGE CORONET R/T

It sits on its nice fat Red Lines like a leech. There's a nasty-looking bulge in the hood, and an insulting rumble out the rear, and underpinnings as stiff as a board to get you going the other way with authority. The instruments are very sanitary. The price, surprisingly modest. The name is Coronet R/T. You can push around town all week, and nobody will know the difference. Except you. And that's what makes the difference.

STANDARD R/T EQUIPMENT
- 440 CID, 375-HP (4-bbl.) V8
- Dual Exhausts
- HD Suspension Package
- HD Brakes
- F70 x 14 Wide-Treads

OPTIONAL
- The Hemi—425 HP

DRIVE SAFELY. IT'S CONTAGIOUS.

Dodge **CHRYSLER** MOTORS CORPORATION

Dodge Scat Pack . . . the cars with the *Bumblebee* stripes

Run with the Dodge Scat Pack

THE CARS WITH THE BUMBLEBEE STRIPES

CORONET R/T
THE TIME MACHINE

Save the competition for the track.
Be a friendly driver.

Coronet R/T. The great-looking, beautifully balanced example of just how easy it is to own the whole show. Beautifully balanced in the engine room, with a 440-cubic-inch Magnum V8 and a TorqueFlite automatic, no less. Superbly balanced at the corners with a special Handling Package that includes an extra leaf in the right rear spring to help put all the torque where it belongs and keep it there. Wide-tread tires and bumblebee stripes, too. And all of these come standard. What's optional on Coronet R/T? Well, among other things, a slick and rugged four-speed manual box. And Dodge's deservedly renowned 426-cubic-inch Hemi V8. The fact that Coronet R/T is also easy on the eyes, strong as a rock, comes in two-door hardtop and convertible versions, and is priced in a very encouraging manner shouldn't hold you back either. With Coronet R/T, everything will stay beautifully in balance, including your budget.

1. DECISIONS, DECISIONS.
Whether to have the bold bumblebee stripe encircling the rear deck, the elegant fine lines running down the flank or perhaps no stripe at all. They are all free. The choice is yours.

2. GENTLEMEN, BE SEATED.
This interior is standard on Coronet R/T. The console and head restraints are optional. But the deep foam padding, the carpets on the floor and that easy-to-keep-great-looking set of buckets are included in every one.

3. YES, YOU CAN.
Order that nifty Rallye dash for your Coronet R/T. Complete with readably round dials, matt black finish, white numbers, and even the full-sized tach and clock.

4. WE'VE GOT YOU CORNERED.
What makes it happen? Plenty. Heavy-duty shocks, springs, a sway bar Charles Atlas couldn't bend, and to keep your rubber on the road an extra leaf in the right rear to control the torque. Also heavy-duty brakes with drums as big as buckets. Front discs are optional for those in a hurry to go nowhere.

No wonder you've got **DODGE fever**

SWINGER

DART SWINGER 340

Play your cards right, and three bills can put you in a whole lot of car this year. Dart Swinger 340. Newest member of the Dodge Scat Pack. You don't make it on looks alone. 340 cubes of high-winding, 4-barrel V8. A 4-speed Hurst on the floor to keep things moving. All the other credentials are in order. Just check below. Then check with your Dodge Dealer. Especially about the price.

STANDARD DART SWINGER 340 EQUIPMENT
• 340-cubic-inch 4-bbl. V8
• 4-speed full synchromesh with Hurst shifter
• Heavy-duty suspension
• Dual exhausts
• D70x14 wide-tread tires
• Dart Swinger bumblebee stripes
• Performance hood with die-cast louvers optional
• 3.23 axle ratio. 3.55 and 3.91 are optional ratios, with Sure Grip differential.

LIFE IS SHORT . . . DON'T MAKE IT SHORTER.
DRIVE SAFELY.

Dodge Scat Pack . . . the cars with the *Bumblebee stripes*

Dodge | CHRYSLER MOTORS CORPORATION

WE'VE GOT YOU CORNERED

CHARGER R/T

We'd like to hand you a line. Right through the esses. And suddenly "sport sedan" takes on an all-new meaning. Wide-treads, heavy-duty springs, shocks, brakes, sway bar. We wouldn't sell a car like this without them. Magnum 440 or optional Hemi. Dodge will see you around.

STANDARD CHARGER R/T EQUIPMENT
• 440-cid Magnum (4-bbl.) V8, 375 hp
• Choice of 3-speed automatic or Hurst 4-speed manual • Dual exhausts
• HD suspension • HD shocks • HD brakes
• Dodge Charger Rallye instrument panel • F70x14 wide-treads

OPTIONAL
• 426 Hemi

DON'T BE CAUGHT DEAD WRONG—DRIVE SAFELY.

Dodge | CHRYSLER MOTORS CORPORATION | *Dodge Scat Pack* . . . the cars with the *Bumblebee stripes*

DODGE CHRYSLER MOTORS CORPORATION

SUPER BEE

CAN LOWER YOUR E.T. AND YOUR PAYMENTS AT THE SAME TIME.

The difference in price between a 1968 Dodge Coronet R/T hardtop and this year's Coronet Super Bee is $215.* The R/T had a 440 Magnum V8 engine vs the Super Bee's 383 Magnum V8, and chrome-tipped exhausts vs paint-tipped pipes. Tests by drag race king Dick Landy with both cars show about a .02 sec. difference through the quarter mile. What to do with the money you save? Try our nasty Ram Air Package (priced at $73.30), quarter scoop panels (priced at $35.80), Sure Grip differential (priced at $42.35), and fat balloons (priced at $26.45), to name a few. That will handle the .02 sec. difference in a hurry.

Coronet R/T. Base car, $3379.00. Rallye instrument panel w/tach, $90.30; head restraints, $43.90. Total, $3513.20. Coronet Super Bee. Base car, $3138.00. Tachometer, $50.15; bucket seats, $100.85; 70-amp-hr battery, $8.40. Total, $3297.40. 4-speed manual transmission with Hurst shifter, heavy-duty suspension, oversize drum brakes, and Red Line tires—standard on both cars.

*Based on Manufacturer's Suggested Retail Price, including federal excise tax and suggested Dealer preparation charge, and excluding state and local taxes, destination charges, and other optional equipment.

Don Garlits tests Challenger R/T:
Says it's "triple tough."

1970 Dodge Challenger R/T

Don "Big Daddy" Garlits, King of the Dragsters, has driven his Dodge Hemi-powered fuel-burning rail to just about every national record and championship in the books. He is truly one of the all-time greats in American automotive competition.

"Now Dodge has gone and done the real thing. Built *the* pony car of all pony cars. They watched the whole pony car thing develop, then built their own super-tough version . . . the Challenger R/T. Compact like a Dart. Wide like a Charger. Just the right size for anyone who likes his own personalized back yard bomb. Dodge should sell a million of 'em. Challenger, and espe-

cially Challenger R/T, are young peoples' cars with young persons' price tags. The standard R/T engine is the 383-cubic-inch Magnum V8, and you can go from there to 440 Magnum and 426-inch Hemi if you want more zap.

"What turned me on is the turning radius . . . it's really tight, which means you get a taut handling package in the stock Challenger.

"Another thing I like is the return to the gauges, you know, gas, oil pressure, amps. No warning lights, but true calibrated gauges on the Challenger R/T.

"Dodge told me that Challenger R/T comes in three body styles. Two-door hardtop, SE hardtop, and convertible. There's loads of options including a four-speed full-synchro transmission and three-speed Torque-Flite automatic with stickshift. And the new colors are something else . . . really wild. The one I drove is 'Go-Mango'.

"Fantastic performance! If I ever leave dragsters, you can be sure I'll run a super stock Challenger R/T.

"If you want to see what Dodge did to pony cars, stop by your Dodge Dealer's and give the Scat Pack Challenger a test drive. You can challenge the world with Challenger R/T."

DIMENSIONS (exterior)
Wheelbase	110
Track, front/rear	59.7/60.7
Overall length	191.3
Overall width	76.1
Overall height	50.9

INTERIOR
Effective headroom	front 38.2 (hardtop)
	rear 36.4 (hardtop)
Legroom	front 42.3 (hardtop)
	rear 30.8 (hardtop)
Shoulder room	front 56.2 (hardtop)
	rear 56.8
Knee room	1.0

CAPACITIES
No. of passengers	4
Fuel tank, gal.	18
Crankcase, qt.	4 (5 when replacing oil filter)

CHASSIS/SUSPENSION
Body/frame type	unitized
Front suspension	torsion bars
Rear suspension	asymmetrical leaf springs

BRAKES—SERVICE
Type	drum, automatic adjusting
Front	11 x 3
Rear	11 x 2½

WHEELS/TIRES
Wheels	14 x 6.0JJ
Tires	F70 x 14 with raised white letters

ENGINE
Type and no. of cyls.	V8
Valve arr.	OHV
Bore and stroke	4.25 x 3.38
Displacement	383
Compression ratio	9.5:1
Fuel req.	premium
Rated BHP @ RPM	335 @ 5200
Rated torque (lbs./ft.) @ RPM	425 @ 3400
Carburetion	4-barrel Holley
Valve train	Hydraulic lifters, pushrods and overhead rocker arms
Cam timing	
Intake duration	268°
Exhaust duration	284°
Exhaust system	dual, reverse-flow mufflers

DRIVE TRAIN
Transmission type	3-speed floor shift standard
Gear ratio	3rd direct 1:1
2nd	1.49:1
1st	2.55:1
Rev.	3.34:1

When he wheeled it out for trial, Don Garlits' Challenger R/T had these additional items of optional equipment aboard: road wheels, racing mirrors, raised-white-letter tires, vinyl roof, and bumper guards.

Charlie Allen tests Swinger 340: Wrings it out good.

1970 Dodge Dart Swinger 340
(all dimensions in inches)

WIDTH	
Track, front	57.4
Track, rear	55.6
Maximum overall car width	69.7
LENGTH	
Wheelbase	111
Overall car length	196.2
HEIGHT	
Overall height	53.0
FRONT COMPARTMENT	
Effective headroom	37.3
Maximum legroom	41.7
Shoulder room	55.4
Hiproom	57.2
REAR COMPARTMENT	
Effective headroom	36.8
Minimum legroom	31.8
Minimum knee room	0.5
Rear compartment room	23.6
Shoulder room	55.4
Hiproom	57.2
LUGGAGE COMPARTMENT	
Position of spare tire storage	floor
Method of holding lid open	torsion bar
ENGINE	
Type and no. of cyls.	V8
Cu.-in. dis.	340
Carburetor	1, 4v
Compression ratio	10.5:1
Transmission	manual 4-speed opt. 3-speed standard
Axle ratio	3.23 (optional 3.55 and 3.91)
Type, no. cyls., valve arr.	90° V8 OHV
Bore and stroke	4.04 x 3.31
Piston displacement, cu.-in.	340
Bore Spacing	4.46
Req. fuel	premium
HP	275 @ 5000
Torque	340 @ 3200
ENGINE PISTONS	
Type	open slipper
CARBURETION SYSTEM	
	Carter AVS-49335
EXHAUST SYSTEM	
	dual, reverse-flow mufflers
DRIVE UNIT	
Synchro mech.	all forward gears
Shift lever location	floor
TRANSMISSION RATIOS (optional 4-speed)	
In 1st	2.47:1
In 2nd	1.91:1
In 3rd	1.39:1
In 4th	1.00:1
In reverse	2.58:1
WHEELS/TIRES	
Type and material	Disc, steel 14 x 5.5
Tires	E70 x 14 fiber-glass-belted bias
BRAKES	
Type	Front disc, proportioning rear, residual pressure
STEERING	
Manual	ratio 24.0:1
Turning radius, curb to curb	37.8

Young Californian, Charlie Allen, has been drag racing funny cars for five years and is already shutting down many of the big names in the game. In his Dodge Dart last year he took 10 major championship wins.

"Save your cash fellas. The giant killer is here. Dart Swinger 340 doesn't have crazy foreign names or cartoon animals plastered all over the side, but that doesn't seem to slow it down much. What it has got is a high revving 340-cubic-inch V8 that nears the 6000 rpm mark. And that's in stock form. The standard job comes with the new MoPar full-synchro, three-speed, floor-mounted gear box. What you get for your dough is a sleek, stiff-sus-pended mini bomb that can show a lot of the high rollers the short way home, provided you do it at a sanctioned meet.

"The one I tested was equipped with an optional Hurst four-speed shifter ... same kind I used in national championship drag racing. This transmission is almost crash proof. I clocked some mighty fine ETs with the stock Swinger 340. In the show department, you can order buckets, hood pins, and lots of show goodies.

"My opinion of the Swinger 340—if you want to put your dough into 'go' instead of mouldings, you'll like it. I do!"

The Dart Swinger 340 Charlie Allen put through its paces carried the following optional, extra-cost items: hood pins, wheel covers, raised-white-letter tires, vinyl roof, front bucket seats, and bumper guards.

Dick Landy tests '70 Super Bee SixPack: Won't give it back.

1970 Dodge Coronet Super Bee
DIMENSIONS

WIDTH	
Track, front	59.7
Track, rear	59.2
Maximum overall car width	76.7
LENGTH	
Wheelbase	117
Overall car length	209.7
HEIGHT	
Overall height	53.0
FRONT COMPARTMENT	
Effective headroom	37.3
Maximum legroom	41.8
Shoulder room	58.1
Hiproom	60.6
REAR COMPARTMENT	
Effective headroom	36.7
Minimum legroom	31.1
Rear comp. room	25.2
Shoulder room	58.1
Hiproom	60.6
CAPACITIES	
No. of passengers	6
Fuel tank, gal	19
Crankcase, qt.	4 (5 when replacing oil filter)
CHASSIS/SUSPENSION	
Body/frame type	unitized
Front suspension	torsion bars
Rear suspension	asymmetrical leaf springs
Steering system	recirculation ball gear
BRAKES—DRUM	
Heavy-duty drum brakes—standard	
Front automatic adjusting	11 x 3
Rear automatic adjusting	11 x 2½
WHEELS/TIRES	
Wheels	14 x 6.0JJ
Sta. tires	F70 x 14 whitewalls
ENGINE	
Type and no. of cyls	V8
Bore and stroke	4.25 x 3.38
Displacement, cu.-in	383
Compression ratio	9.5:1
Fuel req.	premium
Rated BHP @ RPM	335 @ 5200
Rated torque (lbs./ft. @ RPM)	425 @ 3400
Carburetion	4-barrel Holley
Valve train	Hydraulic lifters, pushrods and overhead rocker arms
Cam timing	
Intake duration	268°
Exhaust duration	284°
DRIVE TRAIN	
Transmission type	3-speed floor shift standard
Gear ratio 3rd direct	1:1
2nd	1.49:1
1st	2.55:1
Rev.	3.34:1

Cigar chompin' Dick Landy is a national super stock drag racing champion, driving Darts and Chargers. Holder of Super Stock/F national record and countless track records.

"Let's get one thing straight first. The '70 Dodge Super Bee was designed to provide a full-sized car with a lot of performance and a minimum of ginger-bread. To provide it with stuff that only effects performance. And that's why Super Bee's standard engine is the husky 383-cubic-inch V8 with heads right off the big 440 Magnum which has got to be the hot set up!

"Super Bee is truly the budget super-car for the man who wants a big car performance without spending a bundle for it.

"The Super Bee I tested had the swingin' SixPack setup ... three mind-blowing two-barrel Holley carbs on a new high-rise manifold ... all bolted on the 440 Magnum engine. Biggest problem was getting off the line without smoking it. Feather foot definitely required. The engine, by the way, has had some extra care applied. Optional special cams, mains, and crank. It can take it. The hood has hinges this year, nice when you check the oil, and the scoops feed directly into the Holleys. If the marine-like exhaust rumble doesn't tell you the engine's running, the optional tach will. By the way, I'm not going to give this Super Bee SixPack back to the factory. I'm buying it for my wife. She doesn't care if its clutch-pedal pressure is a little high. She loves the optional, full-synchro, four-speed manual. I told her so."

Dick Landy's Super Bee SixPack test car had the following additional items of extra-cost optional equipment: vinyl top, hood scoops, rocker and sill mouldings, bumper guards, road wheels, front bucket seats, center console, TorqueFlite automatic transmission, and rearview mirror on passenger's side.

This Pony has Horses...
1970 Dodge Challenger R\T

1970's all-new high-performance pony car. It borrowed from no one. Completely new from the wide stance up. And the scoop drops the hint. The pony has a mean streak. Like a 383 Magnum V8. Light it up, and you'll get a quaking trace of four-barrel thunder. Or things get a mite stormier with the optional 440 Magnum V8 . . . or the all-out "haulin' Hemi." Challenger R/T has all the other going goodies, too: 3-on-the-floor full-synchro manual transmission • HD drum-type brakes • Wide-tread tires • Rallye Suspension with sway bar • Rallye Instrument Cluster • Bright dual exhaust tips • 3.23 axle ratio • New longitudinal stripe or traditional bumblebee stripe (your choice) • Brand-new optional 440 SixPack— three Holley two-barrels on a new high-rise manifold, vibrating under the new shaker hood (an option soon to be available). 1970 Dodge Challenger R/T. Kind of "cute" . . . 'til you let out the horses.

Dodge Scat Pack ...the cars with the Bumblebee stripes

Dodge

1971 CHARGER SUPER BEE

The run of the mills is anything but run of the mill.

One great shape. Two great ways to go. First, Charger Super Bee (above), the budget way. Budget, yes—austerity, no. Super Bee's standard mill is the 383 Magnum V8 with free-breathing heads right off the 440 Magnum. It thrives on regular-grade gas and delivers all its energy through a slick, three-speed, all-synchro three-on-the-floor. Yes, Super Bee also has heavy-duty suspension and brakes; Rallye Instrument Cluster; plus

F70x14 wide-tread, whitewall, bias-belted tires; and a bench-type front seat. And what's wrong with that? Now let us proceed to the "all-stops-out" Charger R/T below. This one's a bit different. Its standard mill is the formidable Dodge 440 Magnum—the transmission, the three-speed TorqueFlite automatic. And you know all about them. Charger R/T gives you bucket seats up front, extra-heavy-duty suspension; heavy-duty brakes;

G70x14 wide-tread, raised white letter, bias-belted tires; special paint and stripes. So you see that if you have the urge, we have the Charger for you. Super Bee or R/T. Check your budget again. Then try them both at your nearby Dodge Dealer's. Either way, you can't lose.

Run with the
Dodge Scat Pack

1971 CHARGER R/T

DART SPORT RALLYE.

If you understand what happens when you couple a 2.94 rear end to a wide ratio 4-speed...you're the one we're after.

Dart Sport Rallye wasn't made for those who buy on cubes alone. A super car with a super price, it is not. But boring, dull, or commonplace, it isn't either. The power-to-weight ratio works out to a shade over 20 pounds per horsepower . . . and that puts it in the top 10 percent of the class. The 318 V8 is still the same tractable mill even your maiden aunt could learn to love, but coupled to a new wide ratio 4-speed, it shows a rather refreshing tendency to quickness. The low numeric rear end ratio offers a bonus in effortless super highway travel. Everything

you need is here, the things you don't, aren't. If the list of what you get stirs your interest, hustle down to your nearby Dodge Dealer's. The car's even a little better than it reads.

• 318 V8 with special ratio Hurst-operated 4-speed • 2.94 rear end • Power steering • Rallye suspension • Rallye wheels • E70 x 14 raised white letter tires • Deluxe vinyl seat • "Tuff" steering wheel • Special Dodge lettering on rear quarter panels.

Extra care in engineering makes a difference in Dodge...depend on it.

Plymouth Division

Nationwide Consumer Testing Institute Report:

PLYMOUTH BEATS FORD AND CHEVROLET IN 8 OUT OF 10 OFFICIAL TESTS

Plymouth again proves all-around superiority against its competition. Handling, safety, performance, economy—all of these were measured in the second meeting of Ford, Chevrolet and Plymouth at the Riverside, Cal., course. In a "Showdown" asked for by Plymouth, a 1963 Plymouth Fury V-8 whipped a comparably equipped Chevrolet Impala V-8 and Ford Galaxie "500" V-8 in eight out of ten official tests. Nationwide Consumer Testing Institute bought the cars, hired the drivers, made and _enforced_ the rules. As the chart shows, Plymouth excelled in performance _and_ economy. Add Plymouth's good looks and 5-year/ 50,000-mile warranty*. Plymouth's on the move.

ZERO-TO-SIXTY
PLYMOUTH......11.99 sec.
CHEVROLET......13.64 sec.
FORD...........18.01 sec.

QUARTER-MILE
PLYMOUTH......18.04 sec.
CHEVROLET......18.99 sec.
FORD...........20.53 sec.

KILOMETER RUN
PLYMOUTH......33.43 sec.
CHEVROLET......34.44 sec.
FORD...........37.59 sec.

ECONOMY RUN
PLYMOUTH......18.77 mpg.
CHEVROLET......17.04 mpg.
FORD..........16.14 mpg.

HILL CLIMB
CHEVROLET......15.00 sec.
PLYMOUTH......15.44 sec.
FORD..........**16.00 sec.

CITY PASSING
PLYMOUTH.........278 ft.
CHEVROLET........279 ft.
FORD.............305 ft.

HIGHWAY PASSING
PLYMOUTH.........462 ft.
CHEVROLET........516 ft.
FORD.............554 ft.

EMERGENCY STOP
FORD.............120 ft.
PLYMOUTH.........125 ft.
CHEVROLET........133 ft.

GO-STOP-PARK
PLYMOUTH........2.32 min.
FORD...........2.44 min.
CHEVROLET......2.57 min.

3½-MILE CLASSIC
PLYMOUTH......2:51.74 min.
CHEVROLET......2:55.67 min.
FORD..........3:04.89 min.

**Incomplete third heat   See dealer for full details

*Your Authorized Plymouth-Valiant Dealer's Warranty against defects in material and workmanship on 1963 cars has been expanded to include parts replacement or repair, without charge for required parts or labor, for 5 years or 50,000 miles, whichever comes first, on the engine block, head and internal parts; transmission case and internal parts (excluding manual clutch); torque converter, drive shaft, universal joints (excluding dust covers), rear axle and differential, and rear wheel bearings, provided the vehicle has been serviced at reasonable intervals according to the Plymouth-Valiant Certified Car Care schedules.

PLYMOUTH DIVISION

NOBODY PASSES A NEW PLYMOUTH SPORT FURY WITHOUT THE OWNER'S PERMISSION!

Some folks say this car should come equipped with asbestos gloves, when ordered with the optional 305-hp Golden Commando engine*.

And we'll admit—even with its standard V-8 powerplant—the new Sport Fury *is* one of the hottest cars on the road.

But premium performance is just one of the outstanding features in this limited-production sports model. There are many others that merit your consideration.

King-size bucket seats. Padded dash panel. Torsion-bar suspension. Fully unitized body. Identifying wheel covers. Distinctive exterior trim. Special grille and rear deck design. All are standard equipment on your choice of either model—hardtop or convertible.

Come, take advantage of this special introductory offer: Test-drive a Plymouth Sport Fury and get—free of charge—the biggest boot out of driving you've ever experienced. Your Plymouth-Valiant Dealer will welcome you. One word of caution, however: handle this car with care...it's hot!

---

*Includes dual exhaust, four-barrel carburetor, special high-performance camshaft, high-capacity radiator, heavy-duty, six-leaf rear springs, heavy-duty, 59-ampere-hour battery and dual-breaker distributor.

Leather-like, vinyl bucket seats and daring new rear deck design combine to convince you, this is the one for you. There's no mistaking a new Sport Fury! Hardtop or convertible, the choice is yours. Also available, as optional equipment: Plymouth's Golden Commando 305-hp V-8 powerplant!

PLYMOUTH'S NEW SPORT FURY

There is such a thing as an empty stretch of earth where a man can move a car if he chooses. Just in case you know of such a place, and such a man, we know of such a car. This one.

Sport Fury 2-dr. HT.

For 1964...Get up and go Plymouth!

It's the Sport Fury—by Plymouth! It has the kind of performance that takes you where you want to go the instant you make up your mind. The engine is designed to deliver your kind of road-work. It may be a standard 318- or an optional 361-, 383-, or 426-cu.-in. power plant. You've also a choice between a convertible and a 2-door hardtop version

and your pick of many comfort and convenience options. Sport Fury styling looks good in your driveway, makes you feel proud in mixed traffic. You can be even prouder when you read the engine and drive train warranty.* Test-drive (and buy) a 1964 Plymouth Sport Fury at your nearby Plymouth Dealer's today. Get up and go Plymouth for '64!

*5-YEAR/50,000-MILE WARRANTY— Chrysler Corporation warrants for 5 years or 50,000 miles, whichever comes first, against defects in materials and workmanship and will replace or repair at a Chrysler Motors Corporation Authorized Dealer's place of business, the engine block, head and internal parts, intake manifold, water pump, transmission case and internal parts (excluding manual clutch), torque convertor, drive shaft, universal joints, rear axle and differential, and rear wheel bearings of its 1964 automobiles, provided the owner has the engine oil changed every 3 months or 4,000 miles, whichever comes first, the oil filter replaced every second oil change and the carburetor air filter cleaned every 6 months and replaced every 2 years, and every 6 months furnishes to such a dealer evidence of performance of the required service, and requests the dealer to certify (1) receipt of such evidence and (2) the car's then current mileage.

PLYMOUTH DIVISION ✦ CHRYSLER MOTORS CORPORATION

This is a status symbol. Among people who get excited about things like thermal efficiency, induced turbulence and the flame front.

Plymouth Belvedere Satellites turn up in the strangest hands. Like in the hands of people who will talk your head off over the finer points of cylinder-head design. If that's your kind of language—read on.

Our 426-incher. The Plymouth Commando 426 V-8. 365 hp. This is the wedge-head, street version of our 426 Hemi competition engine that's been making and breaking worldwide dragstrip records. Behind those 365 hp are high-performance valve springs, cam, pistons and plugs. Hydraulic tappets, dual breaker distributor, unsilenced

318-cu.-in. (230 hp.), 361-cu.-in. (265 hp.), 383-cu.-in. (270 and 330 hp.), and then.

The Belvedere Satellite weighs in at 3370 lbs. Think about what happens to its power-to-weight ratio as we bolt on successively brawnier and brawnier power plants. Standard V-8: 273-cu.-in. (180 hp.). Optional V-8s:

air cleaner and dual exhausts.

There are two basic Satellites. Convertible or 2-door hardtop. These features are standard on both: Front bucket seats, center console with glove box, Safety-Rim wheels, custom wheel covers with spinner hubs, torsion-bar suspension.

Plymouth Satellite's a decidedly undemocratic machine. Power-hungry people are the ones it really goes for.

PLYMOUTH DIVISION ✦ CHRYSLER MOTORS CORPORATION

Plymouth

We're big on volumetric efficiency.

That way, our engines stay out front. Along with our cars.

Take the Plymouth Belvedere Satellite above, with its high-performance Plymouth Commando 426 wedge-head V-8. That power plant is the street version of our competition-designed 426 Hemi engine, which holds more records than our competitors care to count.

The Plymouth Satellite's Commando 426 V-8 has high-performance valve springs, cam, pistons and plugs.

Hydraulic tappets, dual breaker distributor, nonsilenced air cleaner, dual exhausts, heavy-duty clutch. And 365 horsepower.

Choose: Satellite hardtop or Satellite convertible. Axles to your driving tastes. Standard engine: 273-cu.-in. V-8. Optional V-8's: The 318, 361's, the 383-cubic-inchers. And, say we immodestly, the optional high-performance Plymouth Commando 426 V-8.

Standard on the Belvedere Satellite are front bucket seats, center console with glove box. Safety-Rim wheels, custom wheel covers with spinner hubs, torsion-bar suspension.

Volumetric efficiency. You can research that one further. Or you can just tool on down to where they're giving free Plymouth Satellite rides. That one's a little easier to find.

PLYMOUTH DIVISION ⬦ CHRYSLER MOTORS CORPORATION

Plymouth

Did you know

that the 1965 Plymouth Barracuda has an optional Formula 'S' sports package that includes a Commando 273-cu.-in. V-8 engine*; heavy-duty shocks, springs, and sway bar; a tachometer; wide-rim (14-in.) wheels, special Blue Streak tires, and simulated bolt-on wheel covers?

You do now.

PLYMOUTH DIVISION ⬦ CHRYSLER MOTORS CORPORATION

THE ROARING '65s
FURY
BELVEDERE
VALIANT
BARRACUDA

Plymouth

Power play.

The new 1966 Plymouth Satellite.

This year, you need a quick eye. Satellite is the newest, hottest Plymouth for '66.

The body is all new. The hypothesis: simplicity. And, look, it worked. Beautifully. Available in hardtop or convertible. Satellite is the top of the Plymouth Belvedere line.

First off, a standard 273-cubic-

inch V-8. Then a whole slew with a fistful of optional V-8s. Transmissions: 3-speed manual, optional 3-speed automatic or manual 4-on-the-floor.

Front bucket seats. Center console with glove box. Special wheel covers with spinner hubs. Deep-pile carpeting. Safety door handles.

Padded instrument panel. Windshield washer. Safety Rim wheels. Curved side windows. And unitized body construction. It's all standard equipment.

Satellite is making tracks in hot-car country. We give you fair warning. With the Plymouth Satellite, something big has come to pass.

 PLYMOUTH DIVISION **CHRYSLER** MOTORS CORPORATION

Let yourself go... *Plymouth*

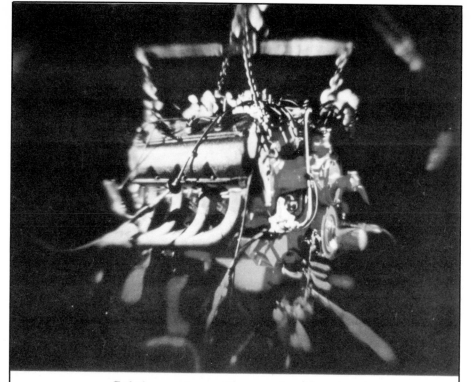

Stick a paper clip on the flywheel and our balancing rig will tell you where it is.

Really. Most other balancing rigs bolt the engine down. Then the test stand usually amplifies or interferes with the engine vibration.

We hang our Hemi engines on a cable and run them so they're free to float (and shake). We detect imbalance with two miniature pick-ups on the front and rear of the engine. They show the exact location and strength of any imbalance.

After that it's pretty easy to add or remove metal in the exact spot

to make the engine dead true. This is a lot of work to go to for a production engine. But it's typical of the way we feel about our cars— the '66 Plymouths.

If you feel that way about great machines (particularly the hot ones), see your Plymouth Dealer and have him show you what we've done to make good-looking cars good movers.

PLYMOUTH DIVISION **CHRYSLER** MOTORS CORPORATION

Plymouth ...a great car by Chrysler Corporation.

'66 Hemi-powered Belvedere . . .

The street Hemi, and how it grew.

The present Hemi head engine design was first introduced in the spring of 1964. Competition use soon proved the great efficiency inherent in the double-rocker, Hemi design. Because of differing racing conditions, two versions of the engine evolved . . . a closed circuit, racing stock car type and a slightly re-tuned model for sanctioned drag racing competition. In short order, the Hemi was cleaning up in almost every sort of automobile competition.

The next step was adapting the engine to normal production cars . . . building the street Hemi. And now the 426 Hemi is available as an option in the '66 Plymouth Belvedere.

**426 inches, 8 barrels,
16 really big valves and 4 rockers.
Get one from your Plymouth Dealer.**

And look what's standard on the Plymouth Belvedere Hemi package. Big brakes . . . 11″ x 3″ front, 11″ x 2.5″ rear . . . 35% more braking area than the standard brake. Complete heavy-duty suspension ; torsion bars, springs, shocks and sway bar. Wide-base, Safety-Rim wheels and high speed tires.

All Belvedere Satellites have bucket seats up front, center console (with the shift lever in the center), padded dash, left outside rear-view mirror and distinctive ornamentation that shows the world you are driving a Hemi-powered Plymouth Belvedere.

Options include rear axle ratios, with our limited-slip differential—Sure-Grip. Your choice of fully synchroed, 4-speed manual or fast-shifting TorqueFlite automatic. Console-mounted tach, front seat shoulder belts (lap belts are standard, front and rear).

And then there's the Hemi engine itself. Aside from some changes to make it operate satisfactorily on the street (like a 10.25 compression ratio so you can use pump gas instead of carrying Av-gas with you, and a choke on the rear primaries so you can start it outdoors in winter), the Belvedere Hemi is very similar to the Hemi set-up of the specially prepared Daytona stockers and the drag strip top eliminators.

Take a look at the chart and you'll see why the Hemi comes on so strong. Like the 2¼″ intake valves . . . that's large enough that a pack of cigarettes will slip through the port !

How the Hemi measures up

ENGINE

Type	90° V
Number of Cylinders	8
Bore	4.250″
Stroke	3.750″
Compression Ratio	10.25
Piston Displacement	426-cubic-inch
Engine Output Horsepower	425 hp @ 6000 rpm
Torque	490 lb-ft @ 4000 rpm

COMBUSTION CHAMBER SPECIFICATIONS

Combustion Chamber Volume	Min. 168 c.c.; Max. 174 c.c.
Distance from Top of Piston to Block Deck	.502″ to .547″
Maximum Variation between Cylinders	.30 psi

CRANKSHAFT AND MAIN BEARINGS

Type	Forged Counter-Balanced, Shot-Peened and Chemically Treated (Hardened Journals)
Bearings	Tri-Metal—copper-lead alloy with steel backing (MS-2356)
Diameter Main Bearing Journal	2.7495″-2.7505″
Diameter Crankpin	2.374″-2.375″

CONNECTING RODS AND BEARINGS

Rods: Type	Drop-Forged "I" beam
Length	6.861″
Weight (less bearing shells)	1084 Grams
Bearings: Type	Tri-Metal—copper-lead alloy with steel backing

VALVES—Intake

Material	Silicon-Chrome X8
Head Diameter	2.25″
Stem Diameter	.309″
Stem-to-Guide Clearance	.002″-.004″
Angle of Seat	45°
Lift	.460″
Lash (Cold)	.028″

VALVES—Exhaust

Material	21-4N Chrome-Manganese with welded stellite face
Head Diameter	1.84″
Stem Diameter	.308″
Stem-to-Guide Clearance	.003″-.005″
Angle of Seat	45°
Lift	.460″
Lash (Cold)	.032″

VALVE SPRINGS

Number	16 (inner), 16 (outer)
Free Length	2.20″ (inner), 2.47″ (outer)
Installed Height	Min. 1.83″; Max. 1.89″
Load when compressed: Valve Closed: inner	47-53 @ 1.635″
outer	102-108 @ 1.86″
Valve Open: inner	86-96 @ 1.175″
outer	179-189 @ 1.40″
Valve Spring Diameter (outer)	1.090″
Surge Damper	Spiral Type

CAMSHAFT—Valve Timing

Intake: Opens (°BTC)	30
Closes (°ABC)	66
Duration-deg	276
Exhaust: Opens (°BBC)	74
Closes (°ATC)	22
Duration-deg	276
Valve opening overlap	52

PISTONS

Type	Domed Forged Aluminum
Material	Extruded Aluminum Alloy, Tin-Coated
Clearance at Top of Skirt	.0025″ to .0035″
Weight	843 Grams

CARBURETOR

Type	Two, 4-bbl Downdraft
Model	AFB-4139S front AFB-4140S rear
Throttle Bore: Primary	1⁷⁄₁₆″
Secondary	1¹¹⁄₁₆″
Main Venturi: Primary	1³⁄₁₆″
Secondary	1⁵⁄₁₆″
Idle Speed (engine hot)	750 rpm
Idle Mixture (both screws only)	1-2 turns

IGNITION SYSTEM

Distributor Type	Double Breaker, Automatic Advance
Basic Timing	12° B. T. C.
Advance—Centrifugal (Crankshaft Degree @ Engine rpm)	0° @ 1000 rpm 3° @ 1400 rpm 17° @ 2800 rpm
Advance Automatic—Vacuum (Distributor Degrees @ Inches of Mercury)	0° @ 6″ to 9″ 4.5° to 7.5° @ 12″ 8.25° to 11° @ 15″
Spark Plugs—Type	N-9Y
—Size	14MM ⅜″ Reach
—Gap	.035″

'67 Belvedere GTX

'67 Belvedere GTX A machine of many talents.

Most assuredly it has an engine. A big wedge-head V-8 at that: 440 cubic inches' worth, with 375 hp. and 480 lbs.-ft. of torque as standard equipment.

It also comes with the street Hemi at 426 cubic inches. The Hemi puts out 425 hp. and 490 lbs.-ft. of torque. (And, of course, costs extra.)

But the nicest thing about the GTX is that it isn't *all* engine. Fact is, it's the most well-rounded Supercar to come out of Detroit (or anywhere, for that matter) in a long time.

Heavy-duty suspension is standard and includes stiffer front torsion bars, beefier ball-joints, heavier front stabilizer bar, firmer shocks and rear springs.

Brakes are big 11 in. drum-type units; although front discs are optionally available.

Tires are special Red Streaks, mounted on 5½ in. rims.

Transmission is through a high-upshift TorqueFlite automatic. But a 4-speed is available as an option.

Other standard GTX items include buckets, hood scoops, low-restriction exhaust system and pit-stop gas filler.

The result is a road machine that not only looks and goes, but one that handles. And steers. And stops. And sticks. It'll do everything but bring you your morning coffee. But with a list of eye-openers like this—who needs it? As you may have heard, Plymouth is out to win you over this year.

Cubic inches aren't everything.

PLYMOUTH DIVISION CHRYSLER MOTORS CORPORATION

The New Belvedere GTX is out to win you over this year.

Supercar.

Supercar. And how! The standard GTX powerplant just happens to be the biggest GT engine in the world. At 440 cu. in., it pumps out 375 hp. and 480 lbs.-ft. of torque.

What's more, the GTX comes with a raft of equipment to complement its under-the-hood prowess: special suspension, brakes, and exhaust system—even a pit-stop gas filler and hood scoops.

Yes, the awesome Hemi is available. With 426 cubes, 425 horses and 490 lbs.-ft. of torque, no less. Still not won over? Come along quietly; we're going for a ride.

'67 Plymouth

PLYMOUTH DIVISION CHRYSLER MOTORS CORPORATION

And why should you? Barracuda, with the optional Formula S road and handling package, is a firm-riding, flat cornering, honest-to-goodness GT car that delights in changing directions.

A look at the package tells why.

In front: high-rate torsion bars, stiffer shocks and a big anti-sway bar. There to control body lean and understeer in corners, nosedive under braking.

In back: heavy-duty six-leaf springs and firmer shocks. Hence wheel hop and spring wind-up under acceleration are all but eliminated, and weight transfer in all directions is further checked.

At each wheel: Red Streak Wide Oval tires. A low profile combined with a low cord angle offers excellent cornering power and wet weather adhesion. Not to mention the ability to withstand hard usage.

At hand: a 4-speed gearbox, if specified. Synchromesh action on all four gears is faultless, with ratios of 2.66, 1.91, 1.39 and 1.00 for flexibility at all speeds.

Underfoot: a 273 or 383 cu. in. V-8. In either case, throttle steering is a simple matter of choosing a line, turning the wheel a mite, and pressing down. Easy. Disc brakes, by the way, are required with the 383, optional with the 273.

Go straight? Sure. Be our guest. But make sure you're in a Barracuda when you do. It's the best means, we think, for getting from one curve to another. Indeed, Plymouth is out to win you over this year. ♥

You'll never want to go straight again.

The new Sports Barracuda. Hardtop and Convertible models also available.

'67 Plymouth Barracuda

PLYMOUTH DIVISION ✦ CHRYSLER MOTORS CORPORATION

'66 NHRA Winternationals, Pomona, Calif.—Shirley "Drag-On Lady" Shahan, in her specially prepared Hemi-Belvedere, shut down all stocks to become the first "Mrs. Stock Eliminator."

'66 NHRA Springnationals, Bristol, Tenn.—Jere Stahl, in a specially prepared Hemi-Belvedere, blew off everybody in A/S, then went on to take Top Stock Eliminator.

We'd like to thank our competition.
For showing up.

Let's just say 1966 was a very good year. For Plymouth, that is. And if you don't believe us, ask the man who didn't own one: he finished second a lot. Which, in a drag race, is about as low as you can get. Too bad, fella. But thanks for showing up.

Moral: Buy The Boss—Belvedere GTX. 440 cubes, standard; 426 Hemi, optional. For street or strip. You'll never love another. Hear us: Plymouth is out to win. ♥

Plymouth

'66 NHRA Summernationals, Indy.—Jere Stahl and said Plymouth did it again, walking away with Top Stock Eliminator (i.e., if you can call an 11.73 ET walking.)

'66 NHRA World Championship Finals, Tulsa—Make that three in a row for ol' Jere, as he and his Plymouth took Top Stock for the third time in one season!

PLYMOUTH DIVISION ✦ CHRYSLER MOTORS CORPORATION

Caught our Strip Show yet?

It's our *Pop Stock Eliminator* contest, and it's the best thing that's hit the strip since the Clan hit 'Vegas'.

In one lane, there's Ronnie Sox and Buddy Martin's race-prepared Boss Hemi-GTX, with 426 cubes, and two 4-barrels. Ronnie Sox is at the stick, and ready to let it happen.

In the other lane, there's a similarly prepared GTX except that it packs Plymouth's waiting 440 cu. in. Wedge, which pumps out 480 lbs.-ft. of torque on a single 4-barrel. The driver is someone you know—and an amateur's amateur. A disc jockey, perhaps. Maybe a friend.

The Christmas tree blinks yellow.... yellow... yellow.... Green.

There they go! Ronnie's spotted the other guy a head start, and it's going to be close. Can an amateur actually beat the Boss? It's happened before, and it can happen again.

And that's just half the show.

The other half we call our *Supercar Clinic.*

Sox & Martin conduct it several nights prior to each contest. Together, Ronnie and Buddy give tips on racing and race-tuning; they show films; they answer questions; they hand out literature; they display the latest in Plymouth speed equipment, and even brew a mean pot of coffee. In short, it's a bull-session. With prizes, no less. And it's free to anyone who likes cars. The root overhead is supplied by your Plymouth dealers, who happen to like cars, too. It's their way of saying Plymouth is out to win you over. ♥

Watch for the Sox & Martin Supercar Clinic and Pop Stock Eliminator contest in your area.

Plymouth CHRYSLER MOTORS CORPORATION

"Beep-Beep!"

©1967 Warner Bros.—Seven Arts, Inc.

You know those cartoons?

About a rapid bird with a "Beep-Beep" voice and a penchant for coyote-squelching?

Right. Name's Road Runner.

Well, Plymouth's built a car with the same name. And personality.

Its horn goes "Beep-Beep!" And the beat goes on. ♥

Road Runner's engine is a special 383 cu. in. V-8, with high-performance heads, cam, 4-barrel and dual exhausts. (There is one engine option. Plymouth's famed 426 Hemi.)

Special body markings warn would-be predators.

And the beat goes on. ♥

Suspension's heavy-duty everything: torsion bars, springs, shocks and stabilizer bar.

Brakes are just plain big.

The body's a lightweight two-door coupe, but it looks like a hardtop.

And we kept the frills to a minimum. So we could do same with the price.

And the beat goes on. ♥

1968

Plymouth

CHRYSLER MOTORS CORPORATION

...the Plymouth win-you-over beat goes on ♥

MOTOR TREND TELLS IT LIKE IT IS...
PLYMOUTH ROAD RUNNER NAMED CAR OF THE YEAR

Several months ago, the staff of *Motor Trend* magazine met in solemn congregation to name the winner of the granddaddy of all car prizes, the 1969 Car of the Year. As always, the award would be given for automotive excellence—to the one car that is most distinguished from its contemporaries. What with the unprecedented number of sizes, shapes, options, and price tags currently served up by the American automobile industry, this year's task was particularly monumental.

Nevertheless, the staff was unanimous in its decision.

The winner just had to be the Plymouth Road Runner.

In one short year since its introduction, Road Runner has advanced a whole new concept in automobiles: that of combining a lightweight two-door body, free of frills, fads and useless ornamentation, with a free-revving engine, firm suspension and heavy-duty brakes. In short, a maximum of machinery, minimum of ostentation and a modicum of price.

It also happens to be an absolute gas to drive, which is another reason the *Motor Trend* Folk named it Car of the Year. It also has to do with the fact that *Car and Driver* magazine rated it number 1 over its five closest competitors.

Hey, maybe the car experts know something you ought to. Why not check out a Road Runner at your Plymouth dealer's? Look what Plymouth's up to now.

"Beep-Beep!"

BEEP-
BEEP!

383

Plymouth   CHRYSLER MOTORS CORPORATION

© Warner Bros.—Seven Arts, Inc.

PLAYBOY: MARCH '69. CAR OF THE YEAR AWARD BROUGHT GREAT PRESTIGE TO THE FANS OF PLYMOUTH'S ROAD RUNNER.

Drift our way sometime.

You're on this big rally, see.

It's getting late and you lost two precious minutes back there in Clydesville when you made that wrong turn, and now you've got to wing it like a big bird if you're going to get back on schedule. Unfortunately, the closed section you're on is not conducive to such foot-on-the-woodery. It's rough as a cob, full of loose gravel and about as straight as a mulberry twig.

In a run-of-the-mill Ponycar, you'd best write it off as an impossible task, resign yourself to finishing 18th, curse the navigator, etc.

But you're not in a run-of-the-mill Ponycar. You're in something special—a new 'Cuda 340. So you nail it.

The 'Cuda responds instantly—big 340 cu. in.

V-8 bellowing, E70's churning, gearbox singing, suspension cushioning, controlling, working. How flat it is as it slides through the turns! And so neutral—Voila!—press on! Grrrrrr! Vrrowwww! Suddenly, before you know it, you've got your two minutes back in hand. 'Cuda 340 is that kind of car. It's capable of being driven very hard without protest. In fact, the 'Cuda carries the same basic suspension as the specially prepared sister-car that won this year's Shell 4000 Rally—the same torsion bars, control arms, anti-sway bar, asymmetrical rear springs, ball-joints—the works. And it's all standard at no extra cost.

The moral? Buy a 'Cuda 340, naturally. And next time, don't make a wrong turn at Clydesville.

Plymouth tells it like it is.

Plymouth   CHRYSLER MOTORS CORPORATION

Plymouth CHRYSLER MOTORS CORPORATION

How do you like your power? Plymouth makes it any way you want. And as new as you want.

We'll make you a car like this 1970 Hemi 'Cuda. With a 426 Hemi engine. (Which is certainly not a run-of-the-mill Mill.) And a "Shaker" on the hood to help our two 4-bbl. carburetors breathe easier.

It's all new.

We slung it two inches lower than last year's Barracuda, pushed the wheels more than three inches farther apart and put on a set of fat tires.

So it crouches.

And it goes as fast as the law allows. (If you're thinking of going faster, remember, we also make cars for the law.)

The 1970 Hemi 'Cuda is part of our whole system of performance cars. From our high-winding Duster 340 (with its low Valiant price, and a super 340 V-8 engine). Right up to the executive Supercar—Sport Fury GT.

Whatever price you put on power, Plymouth makes it.

'Cuda Power

See the 1970 Hemi 'Cuda at your Plymouth Dealer's September 23.

Plymouth CHRYSLER MOTORS CORPORATION

Plymouth Road Runner 2-Door Hardtop

We first introduced Road Runner in '68. It was love at first sight.

A performance car for people who want a car to perform.

A car with a low price for people who haven't stashed away their first million yet.

A car with a personality for people who don't just think of a car as a hunk of iron that moves.

It all clicked. In 1969 *Motor Trend* magazine named Road Runner, "Car of the Year."

For 1970, we present a new Road Runner. We changed it very carefully. In the right places, for the right reasons. For instance, you can order your Road Runner with an all-new, driver-controlled Air Grabber up front. And Road

Runner dust along the side. We think you'll love our Beep-Beep more than ever.

And if you want more to love, look around. We make a whole system of performance cars.

From the high-winding Valiant Duster 340 and all-new Barracuda. To the executive Supercar—Sport Fury GT. Plymouth makes it.

The loved bird.

Road Runner Characters © Warner Bros—Seven Arts, Inc.

The little car that could.

And so it came to pass, from the System that generated Road Runner, the country's first low-cost Supercar—a new scheme, another mind-blowing plan.

Plymouth would introduce Duster 340, the industry's first real Super Compact.

As such, it would have to be more than just a package of add-ons. It would have to be a separate model unto itself, with its own distinct identity, name, bag, schtick—call it what you like.

And aside from that, it would have to meet a stiff list of prerequisites.

First, it would have to move, really move—cut a 13/14-second quarter, pure-stock. Yet, it would have to be powered by a relatively small displacement engine (compacts aren't supposed to be gas hogs, you know). Our light, high-winding 340 cubic-incher would go in as standard equipment.

Second, it would have to handle. Complete heavy-duty underpinnings would be standard, as would slotted road wheels and fat E70 X 14 fiberglass-belted tires.

Third, it would have to stop. Disc brakes would be standard in front.

Above all, it would have to be simple in design and very low in price. The body shell of the new Valiant Coupe would serve admirably. And inside, we'd line it with 4-place bench seating, full instrumentation and a floor-mounted shifter.

At that point, all that remained was to put one together and see if it could meet all those prerequisites.

So we did. And you know what?

It could.

Plymouth CHRYSLER MOTORS CORPORATION

Announcing a new kind of Runner.

Down in Thunder Road country, in the land of the goodolboy and the goodolcar, they speak longingly of the goodoldays and ol' Curtis and ol' Junior and the ol' J-hook and so on.

Some folks would even have you believe the era is still alive.

They say it's come back with an olboy name of Lightning Billy, a young feller who runs his business with computers and slide rules, and how he's the greatest runner of 'em all, and how, on warm nights when the moon is right, you can see Lightning Billy's business coupe, with an enormous wing and a long, pointed snout and great fiery eyes, moaning like a banshee as it sheds the feds in the hills.

Anyway, that's how legend has it. We're not so sure about Lightning Billy, but we do know the car.

It's the new limited-edition Road Runner Superbird, and it marks Plymouth's official re-entry into NASCAR Grand National racing. (Perhaps you remember our exploits in NASCAR: in 1967 we won 31 out of 49 races.)

We're back, and we're glad. It underscores the fact we've got the most comprehensive high-performance program in the industry. It's called the Rapid Transit System, and in it you'll find everything from hot setups like Road Runner, 'Cuda, Duster 340 and Sport Fury GT, to factory tuning manuals and trick parts, all the way to TransAm racers, Super Stockers and AA/Fuel dragsters. There's something for every kind of enthusiast.

So the next time you see a winged Plymouth with a long, pointed snout and a moan like a banshee—and you're not at the Daytona 500—don't think you're seeing things.

Shucks, it might just be ol' Billy on his way home after a hard night's work.

Road Runner Character
© Warner Bros.—Seven Arts, Inc.

Plymouth CHRYSLER

HOT ROD: FEBRUARY '70. JUST HOW BIZARRE WILL DETROIT GO . . . WITNESS HERE THE FABULOUS WINGED SUPER BIRD.

The way Plymouth makes it for 1970

'70 Plymouth Fury.

Exterior Dimensions*		Interior Dimensions***	
Wheelbase	120 in.	Head room, front	38.8 in.
Track, front	62.1 in.	Head room, rear	38.4 in.
Track, rear	62.0 in.	Leg room, front	41.8 in.
Length, overall	214.9 in.	Leg room, rear	38.6 in.
Width, overall	79.6 in.	Shoulder room, front	63.4 in.
Height, overall**	55.8 in.	Shoulder room, rear	62.7 in.

'70 Plymouth Barracuda.

Exterior Dimensions†		Interior Dimensions***†	
Wheelbase	108 in.	Head room, front	37.4 in.
Track, front	59.7 in.	Head room, rear	35.7 in.
Track, rear	61.3 in.	Leg room, front	42.3 in.
Length, overall	186.7 in.	Leg room, rear	29.9 in.
Width, overall	74.7 in.	Shoulder room, front	57.5 in.
Height, overall**	51.0 in.	Shoulder room, rear	55.3 in.

'70 Plymouth Belvedere.

Exterior Dimensions*		Interior Dimensions***	
Wheelbase	116 in.	Head room, front	38.6 in.
Track, front	59.7 in.	Head room, rear	37.4 in.
Track, rear	59.2 in.	Leg room, front	41.9 in.
Length, overall	203.8 in.	Leg room, rear	36.3 in.
Width, overall	76.4 in.	Shoulder room, front	58.1 in.
Height, overall**	54.8 in.	Shoulder room, rear	58.1 in.

'70 Plymouth Valiant.

Exterior Dimensions		Interior Dimensions***	
Wheelbase	108 in.	Head room, front	38.4 in.
Track, front	57.5 in.	Head room, rear	37.3 in.
Track, rear	55.6 in.	Leg room, front	41.7 in.
Length, overall	188.4 in.	Leg room, rear	34.5 in.
Width, overall	69.6 in.	Shoulder room, front	55.4 in.
Height, overall**	54.0 in.	Shoulder room, rear	55.4 in.

*All dimensions listed are for V-8 sedans unless otherwise noted.

**5-passenger load (V-8). ***AMA standard of measurement.
†All dimensions listed are for the Hardtop model with bucket seats.

Standard Safety Features

Rear reflectors and lights • Increased fuel-tank impact protection • Lane-change turn signal • Locking steering wheel • Superior seat belt anchorage • Energy-absorbing steering column and wheel • Energy-absorbing instrument panel • High strength windshield • Energy-absorbing front seat-back and armrests • Seat belts, all seating positions • Shoulder belts, 2 front (except convertibles) • Manual door locks–levers with non-override lock feature, except driver's door • Interlocking door latches • Flush-type inside door release levers • Larger cushioned sun visors • Dual braking system with warning light • Side marker lights • Hazard warning light • Windshield wipers, 2-speed, electric • Vinyl-clad day/night (except Valiant) inside rearview mirror on double-ball-joint mount • Head restraints, 2 front • Locking latch on all folding front seat-backs • Left outside rearview mirror • Flush-type header latch (convertibles) • Fiberglass-belted tires (standard on most models) • Optional safety features: Headlight time-delay • Power door locks • Rear window defogger (except convertibles and wagons) • Shoulder belts, 2 sets, rear (except convertibles) • Disc brakes, front • Tailgate window washer/wiper for wagons • Remote control rearview mirror

	A	B	C	D	E	F	G	H	I	J	K
Engines:	198 Six	225 Six	318 V-8	Commando 340 V-8	Commando 383 V-8	Super Commando 383 V-8	Road Runner 383 V-8	Commando 440 V-8	Super Commando 440 V-8	Super Commando 440 Six-barrel	426 Hemi V-8
Horsepower	125 hp at 4400 rpm	145 hp at 4000 rpm	230 hp at 4400 rpm	275 hp at 5000 rpm	290 hp at 4400 rpm	330 hp at 5000 rpm	335 hp at 5200 rpm	350 hp at 4400 rpm	375 hp at 4600 rpm	390 hp at 4700 rpm	425 hp at 5000 rpm
Torque, lbs.-ft.	180 at 2000 rpm	215 at 2400 rpm	320 at 2000 rpm	340 at 3200 rpm	390 at 2800 rpm	425 at 3200 rpm	425 at 3400 rpm	480 at 2800 rpm	480 at 3200 rpm	490 at 3200 rpm	490 at 4000 rpm
Compression ratio	8.4 to 1	8.4 to 1	8.8 to 1	10.5 to 1	8.7 to 1	9.5 to 1	9.5 to 1	9.7 to 1	9.7 to 1	10.5 to 1	10.25 to 1
Bore, inches	3.40	3.40	3.91	4.04	4.25	4.25	4.25	4.32	4.32	4.32	4.25
Stroke, inches	3.64	4.125	3.31	3.31	3.38	3.38	3.38	3.75	3.75	3.75	3.75
Displacement, cu. in.	198	225	318	340	383	383	383	440	440	440	426
Carburetor type	1-bbl.	1-bbl.	2-bbl.	4-bbl.	2-bbl.	4-bbl.	4-bbl.	4-bbl.	4-bbl.	3, 2-bbl.	2, 4-bbl.
Air cleaner type	Single-Snorkel	Single-Snorkel	Single-Snorkel	Dual-Snorkel	Single-Snorkel	Dual-Snorkel	Dual-Snorkel	Dual-Snorkel	Dual-Snorkel	*Unsilenced	*Unsilenced with Air Grabber
Exhaust	Single	Single	Single	Dual	Single	Dual	Dual	Single	Dual	Dual	Dual
Camshaft	Standard	Standard	Standard	Special	Standard	Standard	Special	Standard	Special	Special	Special
Fuel	Regular	Regular	Regular	Premium	Regular	Premium	Premium	Premium	Premium	Premium	Premium

*Unavailable in California. Availability: Valiant A,B,C,D; Barracuda B,C,D,E,F,G,I,J,K; Belvedere B,C,E,F,G,I,J,K; Fury B,C,E,F,H,J

All product illustrations and specifications are based on authorized information. Although descriptions are believed correct at publication approval, accuracy cannot be guaranteed. Chrysler Motors Corporation reserves the right to make changes from time to time, without notice or obligation, in prices, specifications, colors and materials, and to change or discontinue models.

Plymouth CHRYSLER MOTORS CORPORATION

Plymouth CHRYSLER MOTORS CORPORATION

1970 Sport Fury with new wide stance.

A 1970 Sport Fury. Plymouth makes it. Anyway you want it.

A big car. With a new wide stance. And enough room inside to carry the family to grandmother's house.

A powerful car like Sport Fury GT. With a 440 cu. in. V-8.

A car with a huge trunk. Big enough to carry a two-wheeler home from the store. Or a Christmas tree fresh from the lot.

The kind of car you should have now. The kind of car your kids will want when they grow up.

A car you can make as comfortable as you want. A car like our Brougham model. Soft enough to curl up in the back seat and sleep.

Introducing our newest model.

Plymouth — CHRYSLER MOTORS CORPORATION

The Results:

'CUDA 340

Miles on odometer: 4,220.4
Color: Rallye Red

EQUIPMENT AS TESTED

340 cu. in. V-8 ■ Heavy-duty suspension ■ 11" dia. front and rear brakes ■ 4-speed transmission ■ Performance Axle Package, 3.91:1 ratio ■ Radio ■ Heater ■ Power steering ■ Power brakes ■ Rallye cluster instrument panel ■ Elastomeric front and rear bumpers ■ Bucket seats ■ Console ■ E60 x 15" tires ■ Rallye wheels ■ Road lamps.
WEIGHT AS TESTED: 3,575 lbs.

ACCELERATION

Run #	ET/secs.	Speed/Mph
1.	14.42	98.68
2.	14.78	97.19
3.	14.41	98.79
4.	14.40	98.79
5.	14.81	96.98
6.	14.94 (missed shift)	97.82
7.	14.61	98.36
8.	14.42	98.90
9.	14.40	98.68
10.	14.34	98.79
Average:	14.55	98.30

HANDLING (5 laps, Willow Springs—2.5 miles)

Lap #	Time/min., secs.	Avg. speed
1.	1:52.0	80.36
2.	1:51.0	81.08
3.	1:50.4	81.52
4.	1:49.7	82.04
5.	1:49.5	82.19
Average:	1:50.5	81.45

BRAKING

Stopping distance from 60 mph: 136.8 feet
Weight during brake test (equipment, driver, NHRA observer): 4,010 lbs.

SOX & MARTIN COMMENTS: "Really handles . . . the real sporty car of the bunch . . . 340 really screams . . . mild understeer . . . easiest car to adapt to . . ."

'CUDA 383

Miles on odometer: 407.2
Color: Lemon Twist

EQUIPMENT AS TESTED

383 cu. in. V-8 (std.) ■ Heavy-duty suspension (std.) ■ 11" dia. front and rear brakes (std.) ■ TorqueFlite transmission with SlapStik Shifter ■ Performance Axle Package, 3.91:1 ratio ■ Rallye instrument cluster ■ Rear spoiler ■ Radio ■ Heater ■ Power steering ■ Power brakes ■ Bucket seats ■ Console ■ E60 x 15 tires ■ Rallye wheels ■ Hood pins ■ Side stripes
WEIGHT AS TESTED: 3,575 lbs.

ACCELERATION

Run #	ET/secs.	Speed/Mph
1.	14.45	99.22
2.	14.26	100.11
3.	14.32	99.77
4.	14.32	99.66
5.	14.48	98.46
6.	14.42	99.00
7.	14.42	97.50
8.	14.40	98.79
9.	14.38	98.57
10.	14.42	98.68
Average:	14.39	98.98

HANDLING (5 laps, Willow Springs—2.5 miles)

Lap #	Time/min., secs.	Avg. speed
1.	1:53.4	79.37
2.	1:52.0	80.36
3.	1:51.9	80.43
4.	1:51.3	80.86
5.	1:50.7	81.31
Average:	1:51.9	80.43

BRAKING

Stopping distance from 60 mph: 140.7 feet
Weight during brake test: 4,010 lbs.

SOX & MARTIN COMMENTS: "car just flat runs good . . . SlapStik shifter really gets it done . . . gets around almost as good as the 340 . . . like the color . . . let's eat . . ."

HEMI-'CUDA

Miles on odometer: 637.4.
Color: Rallye Red

EQUIPMENT AS TESTED

426 Hemi V-8 (std.) ■ Extra-heavy-duty suspension (std.) ■ TorqueFlite transmission with SlapStik Shifter ■ Super Track Pak Axle Package, 4.10:1 ratio ■ Shaker hood scoop (std.) ■ Power steering ■ Power brakes ■ Heater ■ Bucket seats (std.) ■ Vinyl roof ■ Elastomeric bumpers ■ Rallye instrument cluster ■ AM/FM stereo ■ Hood pins ■ Road lamps (std.) ■ F60 x 15 tires (std.) ■ Rallye wheels
WEIGHT AS TESTED: 3,825 lbs.

ACCELERATION

Run #	ET/secs.	Speed/Mph
1.	13.67	106.50
2.	13.59	107.01
3.	13.51	107.27
4.	13.63	107.01
5.	13.59	107.01
6.	13.57	106.88
7.	13.39*	108.17*
8.	13.50	107.91
9.	13.46	107.27
10.	13.45	107.52
Average:	13.54	107.26

*Best ET and speed of test

HANDLING (6 laps, Willow Springs—2.5 miles)

Lap #	Time/min., secs.	Avg. speed
1.	1:54.2	78.81
2.	1:53.0	79.65
3.	1:52.9	79.72
4.	1:52.0	80.36
5.	1:52.3	80.14
6.	1:52.0	80.36
Average:	1:52.7	79.86

BRAKING

Stopping distance from 60 mph: 139.3 feet
Weight during brake test: 4,260 lbs.

SOX & MARTIN COMMENTS: "boy, nothing but nothing sounds like a good ol' Hemi . . . a real Hoss . . . carbs flutter just a bit in the turns . . . car understeers a mite, but it feels flat and solid . . ."

ROAD RUNNER 440+6

Miles on odometer: 4,926.6
Color: In-Violet

EQUIPMENT AS TESTED

440 cu. in. V-8 with 3 2-bbl. Holley carburetors (std.) ■ Extra-heavy-duty suspension (std.) ■ TorqueFlite transmission ■ Super Track Pak Axle Package, 4.10:1 ratio ■ Air Grabber ■ Vinyl roof ■ AM/FM stereo ■ Heater ■ Power steering ■ Bucket seats ■ Tachometer ■ Decor package ■ Hood pins ■ F60 x 15 tires (std.) ■ Rallye wheels
WEIGHT AS TESTED: 3,965 lbs.

ACCELERATION

Run #	ET/secs.	Speed/Mph
1.	13.61	105.38
2.	13.71	106.13
3.	13.54	106.13
4.	13.71	105.88
5.	13.65	106.38
6.	13.72	105.75
7.	13.52	106.38
8.	13.47	106.63
9.	13.57	106.63
10.	13.56	105.75
Average:	13.61	106.10

HANDLING (7 laps, Willow Springs—2.5 miles)

Lap #	Time/min., secs.	Avg. speed
1.	1:53.4	79.37
2.	1:52.3	80.14
3.	1:50.6	81.37
4.	1:49.2	82.42
5.	1:49.5	82.20
6.	1:49.0	82.57
7.	1:47.8	83.49***
Average:	1:50.3	81.06

***fastest lap of test

BRAKING

Stopping distance from 60 mph: 136.4 feet
Weight during brake test (driver, observer and equipment): 4,400 lbs.

SOX & MARTIN COMMENTS: Performance-wise, one of the best cars Plymouth offers . . . with the Air Grabber and the Beep-Beep horn, a ball to run around in . . . brakes feel tremendous . . . the 6-barrel is really a sweet motor . . . when do we eat ? . . .

GTX

Miles on odometer: 473.3
Color: Tor-Red

EQUIPMENT AS TESTED

440 cu. in. 4-bbl. V-8 (std.) ■ Heavy-duty suspension (std.) ■ TorqueFlite transmission (std.) ■ Super Track Pak Axle Package, 4.10:1 ratio ■ Air Grabber ■ Console ■ Radio ■ Heater ■ Tachometer ■ Power steering ■ Power brakes ■ Hood pins ■ F60 x 15 tires (std.) ■ Rallye wheels
WEIGHT AS TESTED: 3,795 lbs.

ACCELERATION

Run #	ET/secs.	Speed/Mph
1.	13.57	102.38
2.	13.64	102.85
3.	13.62	103.21
4.	13.63	103.32
5.	13.62	103.32
6.	13.62	103.44
7.	13.61	103.09
8.	13.62	102.97
9.	13.62	102.38
10.	13.64	102.15
Average:	13.62	102.91

HANDLING (5 laps, Willow Springs—2.5 miles)

Lap #	Time/min., secs.	Avg. speed
1.	1:56.9	76.99
2.	1:54.5	78.60
3.	1:53.2	79.51
4.	1:52.6	79.99
5.	1:51.5	80.72
Average:	1:53.8	79.09

BRAKING

Stopping distance from 60 mph: 134.9 feet**
Weight during brake test: 4,230 lbs.

**best stop of test

SOX & MARTIN COMMENTS: very strong and comfortable . . . the family-type Supercar . . . like the dash layout . . . nice finish . . . a quality automobile

DUSTER 340

Miles on odometer: 669.3
Color: Vitamin "C"

EQUIPMENT AS TESTED

340 cu. in. V-8 (std.) ■ Heavy-duty suspension (std.) ■ Front disc brakes (std.) ■ 4-speed transmission ■ Performance Axle Package, 3.91:1 ratio ■ Power brakes ■ Power steering ■ Radio ■ Heater ■ Tachometer ■ Bucket seats ■ Rear-end spoiler ■ Rallye wheels (std.) ■ E70 x 14 tires (std.)
WEIGHT AS TESTED: 3,265 lbs.

ACCELERATION

Run #	ET/secs.	Speed/Mph
1.	14.11	100.11
2.	14.02	100.22
3.	14.00	99.88
4.	14.04	99.66
5.	14.09	100.00
6.	14.18	100.11
7.	13.98	100.33
8.	14.09	100.22
9.	14.07	100.22
10.	14.07	100.11
Average:	14.07	100.09

HANDLING (5 laps, Willow Springs—2.5 miles)

Lap #	Time/min., secs.	Avg. speed
1.	1:52.4	80.07
2.	1:51.2	80.94
3.	1:50.9	81.15
4.	1:49.9	81.89
5.	1:50.1	81.74
Average:	1:50.9	81.15

BRAKING

Stopping distance from 60 mph: 146.3 feet
Weight during brake test: 3,695 lbs.

SOX & MARTIN COMMENTS: I'd like to own this car . . . maneuverable . . . like the way you can hang the tail out . . . nice little car . . . and it doesn't cost much . . . think maybe I'm gonna buy me one . . .

The aforementioned data is certified as correct by the National Hot Rod Association. The information is a measure of vehicle performance on the race track only. Operation of this type where prohibited is strictly discouraged.

The quickest.
(Duster 340)

And the newest.
(Duster Twister)

Aha! Could it be Plymouth has now come through with not one, but *two* Duster Supercars?

Well, not really.

It's just that we've come to the conclusion that the most appropriate way to show off our newest Duster (the Twister) is to show it sitting next to our quickest Duster (the 340).

To look at it, you'd never know that beneath Twister's sleek fastback shell lies one of our 198, 225 or 318 cubic inch engines. The ones that are looked upon with favor by insurance companies, are easy to take care of and don't drink much gas.

Every Twister comes with the unique Duster 340 grille.

It has bias-belted tires and 5½" Rallye wheels without trim rings.

And we've added racing mirrors, flat black hood performance paint, strobe stripes, side stripes, lower deck stripes and optional hood scoops.

Combine all this with torsion-bar suspension (for good handling), solid unibody construction, room for five and an incredibly low price . . . and what more could you want?

The Duster 340, maybe?

The Rapid Transit System. Coming through.

Plymouth

CHRYSLER
MOTORS CORPORATION

Duster 340
Engine: 340 cubic inch V-8.
Bore & Stroke: 4.04 x 3.31.
Compression Ratio: 8.5:1.
Intake System: 4-bbl. carburetor (Thermo Quad). Intake valve diameter—1.88.
Exhaust System: Dual, free-flow headers. Exhaust valve diameter—1.60.
Suspension: Torsion-bar diameter—.87. Sway-bar diameter—.88.
Rear springs (no. of leaves)—6.

Duster
Engine: 225 cubic inch Six (optional).
Bore & Stroke: 3.4 x 4.12.
Compression Ratio: 8.4:1.
Intake System: 2-bbl. carburetor (tuned manifold). Intake valve diameter—1.62.
Exhaust System: Single free-flow header. Exhaust valve diameter—1.36.
Suspension: Torsion-bar diameter—.83. Rear springs (no. of leaves)—5.

There's strength in all our numbers.

There on the left it sits, possibly the best past and present bargain in high-performance cars to ever come along.

The Duster 340.

There on the right sits another bargain. Another Duster.

We build them both pretty much the same way.

The unibody construction is the same. For strength. They both handle the way they do because they both have torsion bars up front and wide-stanced leaf springs in the rear.

A special rust and corrosion resisting process given them is the same.

Yet, the Duster 340 has a few things that other Dusters don't have. Heavy-duty torsion bars. Heavy-duty shocks. Heavy-duty rear springs. A heavy-duty front sway bar. E70 tires. 5-1/2 x 14 wheels. An 8-3/4 axle. And dual exhausts.

The Duster 340's 340 is available with our new Electronic Ignition System.

The system eliminates the points and condenser. Thereby eliminating a major cause of several highly undesirable problems. Point bounce at high r.p.m.s., for instance.

But, for the most part, you can *get* these things with any Duster. Like the heavy-duty suspension.

Or the Electronic Ignition System when you order a 318. Or the big wheels and wide tires.

What this all means is that every Duster we build, be it a 198, 225, 318 or 340 cubic inch Duster, we build with the same result in mind.

To run better than any we've ever built before.

Longer than any we've ever built before. Because we believe that's the kind of car you want. A car built to last.

So pick a number. Any number.

The Rapid Transit System. Coming Through.

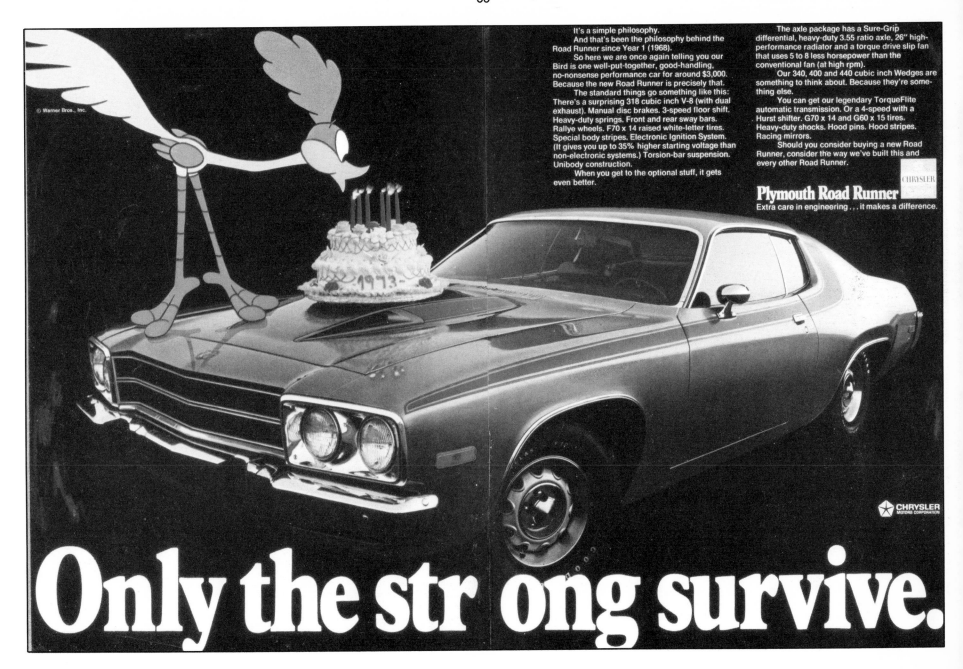

© Warner Bros., Inc.

It's a simple philosophy.
And that's been the philosophy behind the Road Runner since Year 1 (1968).
So here we are once again telling you our Bird is one well-put-together, good-handling, no-nonsense performance car for around $3,000. Because the new Road Runner is precisely that.
The standard things go something like this: There's a surprising 318 cubic inch V-8 (with dual exhaust). Manual disc brakes. 3-speed floor shift. Heavy-duty springs. Front and rear sway bars. Rallye wheels. F70 x 14 raised white-letter tires. Special body stripes. Electronic Ignition System. (It gives you up to 35% higher starting voltage than non-electronic systems.) Torsion-bar suspension. Unibody construction.
When you get to the optional stuff, it gets even better.

The axle package has a Sure-Grip differential, heavy-duty 3.55 ratio axle, 26" high-performance radiator and a torque drive slip fan that uses 5 to 8 less horsepower than the conventional fan (at high rpm).
Our 340, 400 and 440 cubic inch Wedges are something to think about. Because they're something else.
You can get our legendary TorqueFlite automatic transmission. Or a 4-speed with a Hurst shifter. G70 x 14 and G60 x 15 tires. Heavy-duty shocks. Hood pins. Hood stripes. Racing mirrors.
Should you consider buying a new Road Runner, consider the way we've built this and every other Road Runner.

CHRYSLER

Plymouth Road Runner
Extra care in engineering...it makes a difference.

CHRYSLER
MOTORS CORPORATION

Only the str ong survive.

DEPENDS ON HOW FAR YOU WANT TO GO.

AND THIS IS GOING ALL THE WAY.

Every 1974 Plymouth built for performance starts out the same way.

An individual body in search of the body of an individual. You.

Our optional "Tuff" steering wheel. Feels good. Looks good. You can get it on any of our mid-size or compact models.

So an apt description of a performance-equipped Plymouth goes something like this: It's whatever you want it to be.

It's whatever you want it to be because most of the performance equipment we build can go on most Plymouths we build. Dusters as well as Duster 360s. Satellite Sebrings as well as Road Runners. Barracudas as well as 'Cudas.

Naturally, the Road Runner, Duster 360 and 'Cuda offer a bunch as is.

Sway bars. Heavy-duty springs. Floor-mounted, all-synchromesh manual transmissions. Unibody construction. Front torsion bars. And a reputation for performance handed down from the Plymouth heritage of build-

'74 Plymouth standard and optional engines. Our rugged 318 cubic-inch V-8 on the left. Our extraordinary 440 cubic-inch 4-bbl. V-8 on the right. We also have a quick, new 360 cubic-inch V-8, a strong 400 cubic-incher (2-bbl. or 4-bbl.) and a couple of tough six-bangers.

Optional sun roof. You'd love it. Turns your Plymouth into a hardtop convertible of sorts. (Duster sun roof shown. Sun roofs not available on Barracudas or 'Cudas.)

ing good, high-quality, high-performance equipment.

All three cars offer a bunch of options, too.

Performance axle packages (available on Road Runner, and 'Cuda). Special handling package (on Road Runner). 4-speed transmissions with Hurst shifters. Rallye road wheels (standard on Road Runner). Sun roofs (not on 'Cuda). Bigger engines on Road Runner and 'Cuda—up to 440 cubic inches on Road Runner. Bucket seats (standard on 'Cuda). A special soft-rim performance "Tuff" steering wheel (not on 'Cuda). TorqueFlite automatic transmissions. And important little touches such as inside hood releases, racing mirrors and decor packages.

But in each and every case, what we're offering with each and every Plymouth is performance. Performance in terms of equipment you may feel you can do without. And performance in terms of equipment you may feel you can't do without.

Optional 4-speed (with Hurst shifter). If you can handle a 4-speed, this is how to handle a 4-speed.

Bucket seats. These are the great-looking optional all-vinyl buckets you can get on Road Runner. You can also order bucket seats on Duster. Bucket seats are standard on 'Cuda.

Road Runner, Duster 360, 'Cuda
Extra care in engineering . . . it makes a difference.

CHRYSLER Plymouth

CHRYSLER MOTORS CORPORATION

1974 Plymouth 'Cuda

1974 Plymouth Duster 360

1974 Plymouth Road Runner

Chapter Three

Ford Motor Company

Ford Division

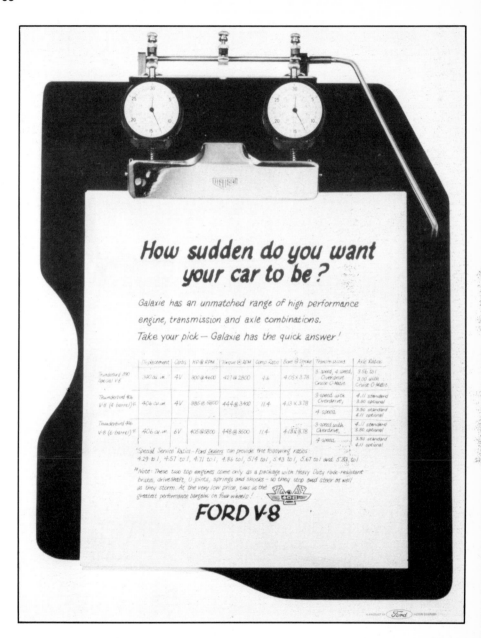

SLEEPER!

To the old carnival guessing game of "Which shell is the pea under?" you can add another—"Which Galaxie is hiding the new six-barrel?"

You can get a very precise answer, it's true, when one of these sleepers suddenly goes "zzz-z-z-ZOW!" and vanishes. But that leaves you sitting foolishly in the middle of a lot of empty landscape.

Better to know beforehand. But how? You'd think 405 horsepower, header exhausts, six-barrel carbs, 406 cubic inches and 11.4 compression couldn't be hidden. But Ford's V-8 magicians have brewed up a real street machine—no wild 2000 r.p.m. idle, no dragster noises, no battle to fire it up. Girls drive these things down to the supermarket and never suspect they are a half-throttle away from escape velocity.

Of course, you do get a clue watching one straighten out a corner. They handle! Because this engine (and the 4-barrel version) come only as a package with Heavy Duty shocks, springs, driveshaft, U-joints, brakes—plus 15-inch wheels and nylon tires. That's what makes the tab of $379.70* so fantastic—and why there are so many Galaxie sleepers around to embarrass you. But why be dominated? Get your own 406 and you won't need to guess which Galaxie has the six-barrel.

*Manufacturer's suggested list price for extra equipment.

FORD V-8

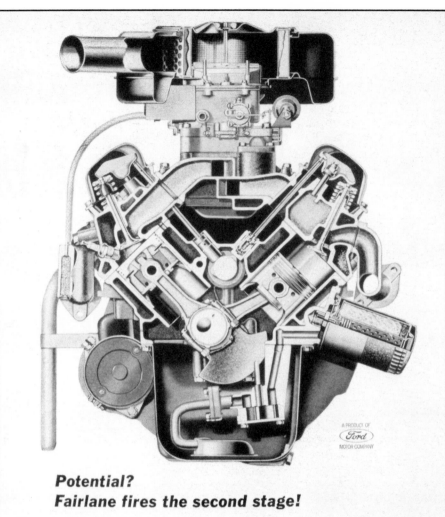

A PRODUCT OF
Ford
MOTOR COMPANY

Potential?
Fairlane fires the second stage!

When engine buffs first saw a cross-section of Fairlane's Challenger 221 V-8 they said: "Aha! Look at all the horses hiding in that little corral!"

And they were right. Because here comes Fairlane with the second stage, hollowed out to 260 cubic inches... and the horsepower has jumped up to a very brisk 164. Torque is a sturdy 258 pounds-feet and (cheers) the diet is still "regular" gas. This extra-cost option, linked to Fairlane's nimble bulk-free size, sizzles out a level of performance that warms any honest citizen's heart.

Of course, there are always the strange ones who can't look at a little gem like this without mentally pulling out the boring bar, the big valves, the "wild" cams, etc. Who can blame them, confronted by this potential, only 20 inches wide across the mani-folds, 27.8 inches long, 465 pounds of precision-molded cast iron—ready to breathe deep and go! Well, let them dream; can we help it if we built a classic?

FORD V-8

Strictly from Stock!

Three times Ak Miller used "all-out" modified engines to top the Unlimited sports cars in the Pikes Peak hill climb. But this year Ak took a new look at the slide rule—and paid Galaxie's rugged 406 V-8 the supreme compliment. He bolted a *strictly stock* 406 into his sports car chassis, didn't even bother to super-tune it—and scrambled to his fourth victory! That same day another 406 in a Galaxie sedan humbled all the other stock cars on the hill. For performance-minded drivers, Ford's achievement is pretty significant: It means you now can get an authentic championship V-8, at *very* reasonable extra cost, right out of the showroom. (No $3000 re-build necessary, thank you.) This one idles like a dynamo, but it puts more pure scat under your foot than you've ever known. Best of all, it comes tucked inside a big, solid, sure-footed Galaxie that's so smooth it's almost wicked. You want to know if a luxury limousine can mate with a sprint car?—see your Ford dealer. He has the quick answer.

America's liveliest, most care-free cars

 FORD
MOTOR COMPANY

FALCON · FAIRLANE · GALAXIE · THUNDERBIRD

Now Fairlane grows four on the floor!

Some drivers (bless 'em) are devout believers in the theory of a great little engine hooked to a great big gear box. For them we have tidings of joy: you now can get a Fairlane V-8 with the option of a four-speed floor shift transmission. This really puts the gem-size V-8 to work, what with four close ratios and synchro all the way. It's a bull of a box, with heft enough for a gravel truck, and it shifts like a pistol shot. Bolted on behind either the 221 or 260 V-8's, the four-speed really puts their potential on tap—and it adds a new luster to Fairlane's nimble handling and neat size. Even if you subscribe to the brute torque philosophy, you ought to sample this combination. Chances are it'll convert you . . . and everybody you pass!

America's liveliest, most care-free cars!

FORD
MOTOR COMPANY

FALCON · FAIRLANE · FORD · THUNDERBIRD

HOT ROD: MARCH '63. WHAT A COINCIDENCE THAT CHEVY ALSO HAD A SIMILAR FOUR-SPEED AD IN THE SAME ISSUE OF *HOT ROD*. CHECK CHEVROLET CHAPTER.

Falcon Sprint V-8: A close look at the world's great new performance car

SPECIAL RALLYE-TYPE woodlike steering wheel, standard on the Sprint, is deep-dished for safety, has the look and feel of wood.

CLOSE-RATIO FOUR-SPEED stick shift is mounted on the floor, gives the 164-hp V-8 an even greater range of performance.

EYE-LEVEL TACHOMETER is on the top of the dash, where the driver doesn't have to take his eyes off the road to read it.

ULTRA-COMPACT V-8 uses Ford-developed foundry technique in cast iron to pare off weight while retaining great durability.

The Sprint is a bold new idea in U. S. automobiles. It combines Falcon's compact size and effortless handling with the kind of V-8 verve that is a Ford speciality...and tops the package off with crisp new scatback styling. Suspension has the sports car accent, too. Extra-duty springs, husky driveline and rear axle, bigger brakes—those were the factors that let the Sprint charge all the way in the Monte Carlo Rallye.

Sprints come only with the new Falcon V-8 engine. Light, super-smooth, efficient, this has 260 cubic inches, 164 horsepower, wears special chrome trim—and sounds like the little tiger it is. A four-speed stick shift is mounted on the floor (optional at extra cost, it will be the choice of most expert drivers). Special wire wheel covers accent the sporting flavor. All in all, a real delight to drive—but very practical, too.

If it's Ford-built, it's built for performance—total performance!

FORD
FALCON • FAIRLANE • FORD • THUNDERBIRD

FOR 60 YEARS THE SYMBOL OF DEPENDABLE PRODUCTS

MOTOR COMPANY

Put away the boring bar—

we've done it for you!

Now we've scooped out Fairlane's V-8 to 289 cubes . . . 271 h.p.! This, friend, is a real stormer! Solid lifters, 4-barrel carb, the whole bit. Can you think of better news for the guy who wants solid, off-the-line punch from a gem-size power plant? Tie this savage little winder to a four-speed floor shift, tuck it into Fairlane's no-fat body shell, and you've got a going-handling combo that's mighty hard to beat...and we mean that both ways! The factory overbore is better than doing it yourself ...you know the cores are in the right place, and the bottom end is tested to take the kind of rpm this V-8 churns out! So put away the boring bar and check your friendly Ford Dealer; he'll show you what 289 cubes can do.

America's liveliest, most care-free cars!

FORD
FALCON • FAIRLANE • FORD • THUNDERBIRD

FOR 60 YEARS THE SYMBOL OF DEPENDABLE PRODUCTS

MOTOR COMPANY

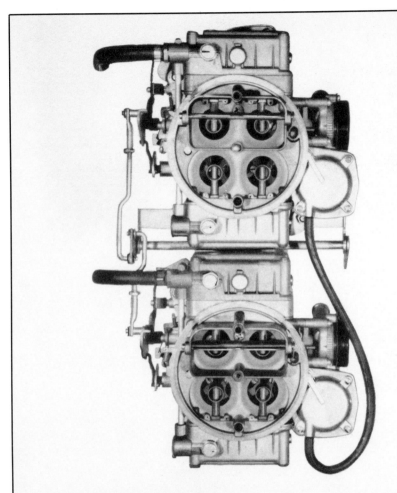

With eight pipes in the organ what noble music it makes!

When you peer down into Ford's big new V-8, this is what you see: The throats of eight carburetor barrels, with a direct pipeline to 427 cubic inches. And when you press the loud-pedal, the noble sound you hear is 425 horses at full gallop. This is the most performance Ford ever built into a car engine, and it can snatch a Ford from zero to 60 so quick you'll think you have amnesia! This one stays buttoned together because the main bearing caps are *cross-bolted*, the crankshaft is electronically balanced to ½ oz. / in.!, the pistons are impact extruded and the con rods look like something out of a Baldwin locomotive. There's a feebler version—a mere 410 h.p. with a single four-barrel carb—but both are stuffed with goodies like solid lifters, a high-volume lube system, aluminum intake manifolds and header exhausts big enough for birds to nest in. Comes with heavy-duty suspension and 15-inch wheels, too. No E. T.'s yet, but what do you want to bet this bear doesn't make history?

A PRODUCT OF *Ford* MOTOR COMPANY

427 cu. in. V-8 high-performance engine by

FORD

COBRAS AREN'T LUCKY...

...They're just the best. Alfred Neubauer, the famous racing manager for the all conquering Mercedes-Benz team of a few years back, was once quoted as saying "successful racing is the elimination of luck." This "elimination of luck" in a championship production sports/racing car is by no means a simple task. A good portion of it, however, can be attributed to the 289 cubic inch "high performance" Ford Fairlane V-8 which powers the COBRA. Although delivering close to 380 h.p. in racing tune the COBRA engine has been one of the most reliable factors contributing toward the COBRA'S fantastic racing success.

COBRAS won all *three* Road Racing Championships open to their class in 1963! The privately entered COBRAS of Johnson and Brown won first and second in the coveted Sports Car Club of America "A" Production Championship. Bob Holbert and Ken Miles placed first and second in the U.S. Road Racing *Drivers Championship* while the COBRA factory racing team won the *United States Road Racing Championship* with a total of 111 points*. What makes this unprecedented display of victory even more impressive is that 1963 was the COBRA'S first year of production! In this one short year the COBRA has proven itself the "Car to Beat" and has become the unparalleled standard by which other production sports cars are judged.

It takes great courage for a relatively small manufacturer (two cars per day) like Shelby American to enter open competition against the best the world has to offer. For on the success or failure of such a venture rides the future of the company. This spirit, however, reflects the dynamic vitality and sound racing experience of that closely knit group of men responsible for the COBRA, for they are the "Eliminators" of that intangible called luck.

*Ferrari 28 pts. Chevrolet 19 pts. Jaguar 12 pts.

COBRA
POWERED BY FORD

SHELBY AMERICAN, INC. 1042 PRINCETON DRIVE, VENICE, CALIFORNIA

Mix a Mustang with a Cobra...

...for the performance rod of the year!

Take these Cobra Kits... slap them on your Mustang 260 or 289 block... and you'll leave the competition sitting in the pits. Whether you're gunning for the quarter or for long-distance runs... there's a Cobra Kit to make your Mustang the hottest performer in town!

PRODUCTS OF (Ford) MOTOR COMPANY

ENGINE PERFORMANCE KIT: Here's a three-way power package for 260 or 289 blocks. Has eight matched pistons with heads designed for valve clearance; high-lift design cam with solid lifters; cylinder head and valve assemblies with heavy-duty rocker arm studs, spring seat ridges, solid valve spring retainers and oil-controlling valve stem seals. Cobra Medallions included. Part #C40Z-6A044-B(260CID), #C40Z-6A044-C(289). Each $345.25*

THREE 2-V INDUCTION KIT: Match this kit with the distributor and engine performance kits and watch the horses soar! Kit has three 2-V carburetors on cast-aluminum intake manifold, special air cleaner. Mechanical linkage lets you "go on one" for economy, cut in the other two for maximum go under high-performance conditions. Cobra medallions also included. Part #C40Z-6B068-A (260CID), #C40Z-6B0-68-B(289). Each $212.55*

DISTRIBUTOR KIT: This high-performance kit consists of heavy-duty distributor and leads. Features dual points, centrifugal spark advance. Use the kit to give your engine the high-speed performance characteristics you want that are especially suited for drag strip operations and other high RPM requirements. Part #C4DZ-12050-A. $49.80*

HEAVY-DUTY CLUTCH KIT: This kit consists of disc assembly and pressure plate. Construction of both the plate and disc assembly virtually eliminates slipping and provides maximum performance under demanding conditions. Part #C30Z-7A537-A. $51.45*

*Manufacturer's suggested retail price. Installation and state or local taxes, if any, are extra.

These are just a sample of the Cobra Kits for Mustangs you can get from your Ford Dealer

Now we've added a 2+2 to the Mustang stable

If that slippery shape makes everything else within a half mile look homemade—too bad. That's progress.

Well, they still have Lollobrigida... and Chateau Mouton Rothschild '59 and Balenciaga. But Europe no longer has a monopoly on this kind of four-wheeled flair and fire. Not with the Mustang 2+2 suddenly appearing on the scene. Just think, an unexpected low price and options you can't get in Modena and 6,000-mile or 6 months' maintenance and a ride like a little fat cloud and service at any Ford Dealer's.

Speaking of options, the basic V-8 has 289 cubes and 200 horsepower; the No. 2 version has a four-barrel carburetor and 225 hp. (but still with hydraulic lifters) and the solid-lifter High Performance jewel turns out 271 horses. Unless you want to go the kit route and that climbs all the way up to four Webers and 330 beasts (can you call 'em horses?).

More good news: front disc brakes are available, and for very little scratch. But the 2+2's fold-down rear seat, which opens up a ski-length luggage area right back to the trunk sill, isn't an option, it's there for free. And so are the bucket seats and floor-shift levers and the 200 cubic

inches in the six-cylinder engine. And the looks. Don't forget the looks: that's what turns Main Street into the Via Veneto... and you into Nuvolari!

Best year yet to go Ford
Test Drive
Total Performance '65

A PRODUCT OF (Ford) MOTOR COMPANY

The Total Performance Ford Galaxie 500/XL Hardtop

On the pad!

Don't let the look of cool elegance give you any false ideas about the character of these '65 Fords; that sculptured metal covers the hottest road missile you can find in any U.S. showroom.

You like a real fire-breather, something that turns on four-alarm response the split second you blip the throttle? How can you do better than Ford's high-performance V-8? Displacement is 427 cubic inches, horsepower 425—but you can't get this V-8 without the heavier-duty suspension, and tires that make the road-holding as "sticky" as the engine is strong. (We won't sell 'em any other way, but people seem to like the thought—we've made more of these scorchers than all the other makers put together.)

Back to that cool look; maybe it does say something about the character after all. Because these are wonderfully quiet and docile for such white-hot performance...and with the liquid-satin ride of Ford's new full-coil suspension they cruise like an Atlas in orbit. If you choose to tread lightly, your passengers need never know about that fire under the hood. (But you will!)

Best year yet to go Ford!
Test Drive Total Performance 65

A PRODUCT OF
MOTOR COMPANY

THE TOTAL PERFORMANCE FORD FAIRLANE 500 SPORTS COUPE (BUCKET SEATS) STANDARD

Is Fairlane as quick as it looks?

Ask Carroll Shelby who builds the Cobra sports car. He says Fairlane's 289 cu. in. V-8 option is the "best V-8 ever to come out of Detroit." *Or ask any Fairlane owner...*about Fairlane's sporty optional features. 4-speed stick. Overdrive. Tachometer. You name it. How much? Never before has so little money bought so much car. Ask any Ford Dealer.

Best year yet to go Ford!
Test Drive Total Performance 65

FORD
MUSTANG · FALCON · FAIRLANE
FORD · THUNDERBIRD

Here's what can happen when you build a foundry too close to a Swiss cheese factory

You get giant holes in your intake manifold. So the only solution is to bolt eight-barrel carburetion on top and tuck a Ford 427 block underneath, and cop the title of World's Strongest Sandwich (stock division).

Seriously, this is merely a reminder that Ford doesn't stand still, even with a great engine like the 427 High Performance V-8. Peel one open now and you'll find *machined* combustion chambers, a lighter weight valve train, bigger and lighter hollow-stemmed valves, a forged steel crank with hollow crankpins, stronger con rods, pop-up pistons and a huge oil gallery low in the block (which also is new) that feeds oil directly to the main bearings.

No big engine has a right to rev the way this one does—

but it does and it stays stuck together. Better still, you don't have to be an insider to get one of the good ones; this is a John Citizen engine. It goes the way it goes right off the showroom floor.

As always, Ford wraps this one up with heavy-duty springs, shocks, wheels and tires to match. That's just good sense, but it also makes an unbeatable combination. If you want to know how a vegetarian feels the day he discovers steak, just try it! Some sandwich!

Best year yet to go Ford!
Test Drive Total Performance '65

FORD
MUSTANG · FALCON · FAIRLANE
FORD · THUNDERBIRD
PRESENTS OF Ford

How to make an Italian cry

Tell him the fantastic Shelby G.T. 350 is America's answer to all those terrible-tempered Italian sports cars. Then show him. Bred by Cobra, powered by Ford, designed by Commendatore Carroll Shelby... the G.T. 350 is a car that sounds like a car and goes with all the spirit and speed of a competitor. The engine starts as a brute-force Ford 289 and then the Commendatore goes to work... four-barrel carburation, high-rise aluminum manifold and a hand-built tuned exhaust system...the end result is 306 horses. The "four on the floor" is a fully synchronized Sebring close ratio transmission that shifts like butter and grabs like a vise. The entire G.T. 350 suspension is computer designed...front anti-roll bar, competition shock absorbers, front disc brakes, torque controlled rear axle. And she sits (goes) on 130 mph Goodyear Blue Dot tires. For excitement add the new rear quarter panel windows and sleek rear brake air scoops. Price? $4428 plus taxes and transportation. Get behind that racing steering wheel. Pinch it and she really goes. Bono vita!!!!

SHELBY G.T. 350

1966 Fairlane GT

The great thing about Fairlane's new GT/A automatic is it can stop being automatic.

Comes a time in the life of every manual shift when you wish you had an automatic transmission. Comes also a time in the life of every automatic transmission when you wish you had a manual shift.

What a perfect time to spring the new Fairlane GT/A Sportshift.

This Fairlane option gives *you* the option of automatic convenience or manual fun. It also gives you a 335-horsepower V-8, which lifts it out of the Amusing Gadget class fast.

Under the GT/A's console mounted T-handle selector is a quadrant reading "P-R-N-D-2-1." Through the P-R-N-D part it's pure automatic.

Makes all the shifting decisions for you. But flick into 1 or 2 and it's your move. You decide how long to hold it and when to shift. Here in

one fell swoop is manual gearbox flexibility with the ease of automatic drive only a shift away.

What you can accomplish with a 390-cubic-inch hydraulic lifter V-8 harnessed to this GT/A setup—and packed into Fairlane's trim dimensions—is something you'll have to work out with your imagination.

Progress, it's wonderful. Sportshift, it's unbelievable—until you try it.

AMERICA'S
TOTAL PERFORMANCE CARS

FORD
MUSTANG · FALCON · FAIRLANE
FORD · THUNDERBIRD

1966 Ford 7-Litre Hardtop

Ford 7-Litre...either the quickest quiet car or the quietest quick car

Well, once again we've invented a new kind of car. It's not a competition car (that's why the overbore to 7 litres/428 cubic inches.) But it turns on like a competition car (after all, 462 pounds/feet of torque!) What it is is lightning without thunder. It *moves*—but it moves like mist over a millpond, smoothly, quietly, effortlessly!

It *stops*, too! Power disc brakes up front are standard. So are bucket seats. The V-8 comes in just one size, with a 4-barrel car-

buretor and the beefy bottom end that is the heritage of Ford's tremendous competition program. But the lifters are hydraulic for silence' sake and even the dual exhausts are very discreet. You get your choice of convertible or two-door hardtop, four-on-the-floor or Cruise-O-Matic . . . and just about any other added pleasure Ford makes, including air conditioning.

You'll have to decide whether it's a cool hot car or a hot cool car. But one thing you're bound to decide—there just isn't anything else like it!

AMERICA'S
TOTAL PERFORMANCE CARS

FORD
MUSTANG · FALCON · FAIRLANE
FORD · THUNDERBIRD

Big gun for tiger country, Fairlane GT!

This sleek, wild, new Fairlane GT comes loaded. It's loaded with bucket seats, big 390 cubic-inch V-8 engine, console-mounted gear shift, special hood "louvers", GT paint stripes, and more (all standard). Just what you need to dust off a tiger.

Just what you need for the most exciting driving you've ever known!

If you want your GT automatic, there's a special treat in Fairlane GT/A with Sport Shift. Sport Shift gives you "P, R, N, D"—just like any automatic. And

it acts just like any automatic as long as you leave it in "D." But—Sport Shift also has "1" and "2" below "D," and these two positions act like first and second gear in a manual—except you don't have to bother with a clutch. So you get all the fun and sure control of a manual with the convenience of an automatic (a very shifty proposition).

If you want a big gun for tiger country, maybe it's time for Fairlane GT. But, watch it. Fairlane GT comes loaded.

AMERICA'S TOTAL PERFORMANCE CARS

FORD

MUSTANG · FALCON · FAIRLANE
FORD · THUNDERBIRD

1966 Fairlane GT Hardtop

Fairlane GT...powerful medicine for those dull driving blues. Standard prescription on the GT includes a hefty 390-cubic-inch V-8, all-vinyl bucket seats, GT stripes, and a console-mounted, fully synchronized stick shift, all blended to make you feel *good* in a hurry.

If you need a more special treatment, turn your Fairlane into a GT/A. Secret ingredient in this tonic is the Sport Shift, it can be fully automatic, or you can shift it through the gears—as you choose. One dose of this Fairlane and you'll never feel sluggish again.

Pop yourself and the kids into one of these capsules—Fairlane GT or GT/A convertible or hardtop. And see what Fairlane-type performance will do for your metabolism.

YOU'RE AHEAD
IN A FORD
ALL THE WAY!

FAIRLANE

See your Ford Dealer now during his Spring Sports Sale

PLAYBOY: FEBRUARY '66. THIS GT NOT ONLY HUNTED PONTIAC TIGERS, IT BAGGED ITSELF A BUNNY.

LIFE: **APRIL 29, 1966. "POP YOURSELF CAPSULES—POWERFUL MEDICINE FOR THE BLUES." STRANGE LANGUAGE FROM AN AUTO COMPANY.**

All-new for '67:
Fairlane Ranchero
with Thunderbird thunder.

Right from the first look you know something wonderful's happened to Ranchero. It's longer, leaner, with all the promise of excitement you'd expect in a Fairlane. And how Ranchero delivers on that promise! It begins with an optional 390-cubic-inch Thunderbird V-8 — just one of four engines available. Add a fully synchronized four-speed transmission with floor shift — or SelectShift Cruise-O-Matic, that gives you the convenience and the fun of both manual and completely automatic shifting. Complete the picture with individually adjustable, contoured bucket seats, center console, radio/stereo-sonic tape system, and air conditioning. And for the greatest thrill, check Ranchero's price tag. It's the one thing about this beauty that's not big, bold and luxurious. **Fairlane Ranchero/67**

Go automatic—or shift for yourself. New optional SelectShift Cruise-O-Matic allows you to do both • Center: handsome interior of Fairlane Ranchero 500XL, one of three models available • Roomy 6½-foot box with double-wall sides for added strength, one-hand tailgate latch for easy operation. Overall Ranchero load capacity now up to 1250 pounds.

Ford

You're ahead in a Ford.

---

want
more
F.P.M.?*
try a Shelby GT

*That's Fun-Per-Mile—yours aplenty in these *two* great new GT cars from Shelby American.

There's more F.P.M. when you have reserve performance. The GT 350 carries a 306 horsepower 289 cubic inch V-8. The GT 500 is powered by the 428 cubic inch V-8, descended from the 1966 LeMans winning Ford GT.

The F.P.M. is higher when steering is competition-quick, suspension is firm. Driving's *fun* with the safety of an integral roll bar, shoulder harnesses, disc front and drum rear brakes, wide-path 4-ply nylon tires.

Driving's *fun* with the Shelby brand of comfort and style. For more F.P.M., see your Shelby dealer P.D.Q.

SHELBY G.T. *350 and 500* **The Road Cars** Powered by *Ford*

Shelby American, Inc., 6501 W. Imperial Highway, Los Angeles 90009

"GO LIKE A CHAMPION"
with the equipment of the Champion

Every part in the Cobra High Performance line has been race tested and proven by the Shelby American Racing Team. Shelby American earned the World Manufacturers Racing Championship in 1965 with the Cobra and prepared the Ford GT Mark II coupes that finished 1 - 2 at Le Mans in 1966.

$34.50

Cobra Tachometer: Three inch diameter, 250° sweep, 0-9000 electrical tachometer provides maximum accuracy. Internally lighted and completely self-contained; no sending unit required. Easy installation on all cars.

$29.95

Cobra Aluminum Valve Covers: The real thing—used on all Cobra engines. Kit includes gaskets, bolts, and instructions; internal baffles & breather tube already installed.

$249.50

Dual Quad High Riser Induction: 40-50 hp increase. Kit includes two Holley 460 carburetors, progressive linkage, fuel log, air cleaner, gaskets, and fittings.

"Tuned" Exhaust Headers: $110.00—Gives more hp and higher rpm. Complete system, with mufflers and tailpipes, is $152.95.

Cam & Tappet Set: This cam made the 289 Cobra famous. Adds over 25 hp; ideal for street and race. Cam, Tappets and Springs. $59.95.

Send this coupon today for the name of your nearest Dealer.

To: Shelby American, Inc.—Dept. C-120
6501 West Imperial Highway
Los Angeles, California 90009

NAME

ADDRESS

CITY

STATE _____ ZIP

☐ Please send the name of my local Cobra Kit franchised dealer.

☐ $1.00 enclosed for the new Cobra Kit parts catalogue, tuning tips and Cobra decal.

COBRA KITS

Designed exclusively for Fords by Ford experts.

Order your Mustang as hot as you like

...even Shelby hot!

There's a GT package for every kind of Mustang. From the 289- to the 390-cu. in. V-8 and you choose pure stick shifting or SelectShift fully automatic/fully manual.

Every Mustang GT sits firmly on special wide oval tires, plus higher-rate springs, shocks, and stabilizer bar, GT stripes, natch, four-inch fogs, and front power discs, too.

Want more? There's always Mr. Shelby's sizzling Mustang-based GT 350. Above, Mr. Shelby with his GT 500—Le Mans developed 428-cu. in., modified front suspension, four-leaf rear springs. And all the standard Mustang GT features. Order your Mustang as hot as you like. Every Ford Dealer can get you a Mustang GT; many handle the Shelby cars. And you can add almost any extras, all the way to stereo tape. That way, even a hot Mustang can keep its cool.

THE ORIGINAL

MUSTANG

1968 Torino GT fastback's only concession to convention is six-passenger seating, if you prefer.

Anyone can paint stripes on a car...we earned ours at Le Mans...Sebring... Indianapolis...

When you go fastback or GT... you've got to go Ford! And one of the reasons why is the newest member of Ford's winning fastback pack, the Torino GT. Built on a 116-inch wheelbase, this one sports such standard equipment items as a 302-cu. in. V-8, SelectShift transmission, unique GT stripes and identification, styled steel wheels and wide-oval tires.

But, Ford didn't stop with one well-bred fastback, it went on to make an entire pack . . . five models in three different sizes . . . small, medium, and large. Ford calls them the Mustang Fastback 2+2, Torino GT fastback, Fairlane 500 fastback, Ford XL fastback and Ford Galaxie 500 fastback. People who consider driving a sport call them great. The reasons why are as varied as the selection of models and options.

Consider five different V-8's for the XL. These run all the way from a new 302-cu. in. jewel with special light-weight pistons, to the proven 428-cu. in. V-8. These range from 210 to 390 hp. With five V-8's each for Torino, Fairlane and Mustang, the fastback pack really lays on V-8 choice.

They're not stinting on transmissions either. On most of these engines you can have either 3-speed, 4-speed, or syrup-smooth 3-range SelectShift. That's the automatic that leaves the option to shift or not to shift up to you. Ford doesn't let you build in all this go without having something special in the stop department. That something is a new optional floating-caliper disc brake that quickly disperses heat for high fade resistance, more uniform braking action.

There are eight V-8's, three transmissions, two suspensions, three tire options, two brake setups and five models . . . if your choice is GT or fastback, is there any doubt that Ford gives you the biggest choice? There's no need to choose things like stripes, low-restriction exhaust, and special wheel covers . . . Ford includes these in the special GT packages available for both Ford and Mustang.

If there's a fastback in this mix with your name on it, the nicest surprise is yet to come. Just because it's pretty doesn't mean that Ford is going to twist your arm. You'll see what we mean when you check the price tag. Get the message? Ford did . . . loud and clear.

FORD ...has a better idea.

HORIZON GRABBER

Ford knows that great road cars are made, not born. Case in point: 1968 XL Fastback. You can make it 428 cubic inches big, to take the measure of a long, black line on the salt or snake over the purple mountains in the distance. Optional front disc brakes, heavy-duty suspension, SelectShift (answers the question—to shift or not to shift?) are just a few of the other reasons why big Ford can live on any road you can find. There's a lot more to it than just some finely engineered components, though. Big Ford was built to be a driver's car right from the optional equipment wide-oval tires up. There's a unit-built body shell—almost strong enough to be a car all by itself—mounted on a computer-designed separate chassis. This Ford-engineered combo swings just enough so that wheels and suspension handle the rough stuff instead of just skittering sloppily over it. Try that long, open bend, the washboardy one that's the terror of every hard-sprung sports car in the neighborhood. The third or fourth time through it in the big Dearborn Delight and you'll realize Ford engineering has been there before . . . thousands of times. That's how our slide-rule brigade learns about great road cars.

Some nuts-and-bolts facts about the '68 Fords: you can choose from five V-8's from 302 to 428 cubic inches. Three- and four-speed manual transmissions...plus the 3-speed SelectShift automatic. Two different suspensions: stock and heavy-duty. Power front disc brakes, and wide-oval or radial-ply tires. Fourteen convertible, sedan and hardtop models...plus seven wagon models.

Carroll Shelby designed his COBRA GT to go like it looks

A brand-new Ford 302 cubic inch V-8 delivers for the GT 350. On the GT 500, a Ford 428 cubic inch V-8 is standard, with a new 427 V-8 powerhouse as a super-performance option. ☐ Four-speed transmissions are standard, close-coupled automatics are low-cost options. ☐ Great handling comes from competition-engineered suspension, 16-to-1 ratio power steering, adjustable shocks, heavy duty driveline and rear axle, and special high performance 130-MPH rated nylon tires. Front disc brakes, of course. ☐ And with this superb performance, Cobra GTs deliver head-turning styling *and* luxury, too. ☐ Interiors gleam with unique simulated wood grain trim on instrument panel, steering wheel, console and door panels. ☐ The exterior styling features *work* for you. ☐ Hood scoops supply extra carburetor air, fastback louvers are air extractors. ☐ Safety has not been overlooked—wide-rim wheels, integral overhead bar and shoulder harnesses are included. ☐ Carroll Shelby's unique fastbacks and new-for-'68 convertibles, are design-based on the Mustang, winner of two consecutive Trans-Am road racing championships. ☐ And that means real economy, a surprisingly low price for you. ☐ All four Cobra GTs say "Let's go!" ☐ See your Shelby Cobra dealer—and get going!

Shelby COBRA GT 350/500   POWER BY Ford

1969 Cobra SportsRoof

1969 Cobra Hardtop with 428 CID 4V Cobra Jet Ram-Air V-8 option.

Cobra Specifications—*Standard engine:* 428 CID 4V V-8. Bore and stroke, 4.13 x 3.98 in. 10.6:1 compression, premium fuel. 335 hp at 5200 rpm. Torque 440 lbs-ft at 3400 rpm. Ram-Air induction optional. *Transmissions:* 4-speed manual; ratios: 2.72:1, 1.89:1, 1.29:1, 1.00:1. Optional SelectShift (floor shift with optional console), ratios: 2.46:1, 1.46:1, 1.00:1. *Rear Axle* ratio: 3.25:1 standard (3.45, 3.91, 4.30 optional). *Brakes:* 10.0 in. drums, lining area 173.3 sq. in. Optional power front disc brakes, total swept area 232.0 sq. in.

Torino GT Specifications—*Standard engine:* 302 CID 2V V-8. Bore and stroke, 4.00 x 3.00 in. 9.5:1 compression, regular fuel. 220 hp at 4600 rpm. Torque 300 lb. at 2600 rpm. *Optional engines:* 351 CID 2V or 4V V-8 (see page P4), 390 CID 4V V-8 (see page P6), 428 CID V-8 (see Cobra specifications). All 4V optional engines have dual exhausts. *Transmissions:* Std. 3-speed, fully synchronized, ratios: 2.99:1, 1.75:1, 1.00:1. Optional, 4-speed floor shift fully synchronized, ratios: 2.78:1, 1.93:1, 1.36:1, 1.00:1; SelectShift Cruise-O-Matic, ratios 2.46:1, 1.46:1, 1.00:1. *Brakes:* 10.0 in. drums, lining area 173.3 sq. in., optional power front disc brakes, total swept area 232.0 sq. in. *Wheelbase:* 116". Overall length 201.1". Weights, hardtop 3327, con-

Wheelbase: 116". Overall length 201.1". Weights, hardtop 3633, SportsRoof 3689 lb. *Wheels:* 14", 6" rim, F70-14 wide-tread belted tires. *Suspension:* Competition HD. **Cobra Options:** 4V Cobra Jet Ram-Air V-8 with functional hood scoop—$133.44 over base 428 V-8 • F70 x 14 Wide-Oval Belted Tires, raised letter (required with 428 Cobra Jet Ram-Air)—$13.05 • Power Front Disc Brakes—$64.77 • Traction-Lok Differential—$63.51 • Bucket Seats—$120.59 • 6000 rpm Tachometer—$47.92 • SelectShift Cruise-O-Matic—$37.06.*

vertible 3510, SportsRoof 3374 lb. *Wheels:* 14" styled steel, 6" rim, E70X14 wide-tread belted with 302 and 351 V-8's; F70X14 with 390 and 428 V-8's. *Suspension:* GT handling. **Torino GT Options:** Extra charge over 302 CID V-8: 351 CID 2V V-8 (250 hp)—$58.34; 351 CID 4V V-8 (290 hp)—$84.25; 390 CID 4V V-8 (320 hp) (requires optional transmission at extra cost) —$163.24; 428 CID 4V V-8 (335 hp)—$287.53; 428 CID 4V Cobra Jet Ram-Air V-8 (335 hp) (all 428 CID V-8's require Cruise-O-Matic or close ratio 4-speed transmission at extra cost)—$420.96 • 4-Speed Manual Transmission (not available with 302 CID V-8)—$194.31 • SelectShift Cruise-O-Matic w/302 & 351 2V or 4V V-8's—$200.85; 390 & 428 4V V-8's—$222.08 • Bucket Seats—$120.59.*

COBRA

COBRA–raised in a tough neighborhood! (Daytona, Riverside, Atlanta)

Here's the nearest thing to a NASCAR stocker you can bolt a license plate onto. It's got a body frame structure and chassis designed to win time after time under brutal pounding in the bullrings of North Carolina, to outhandle the competition in the tortuous bends of the Riverside 500, and burn the Daytona backstretch at 190. You've never seen so much performance per dollar before. The formula is simple—we put the money in the muscle, like a standard 4V 428 CID V-8. It's rated at 335 horsepower conservatively. And there's a chassis to match the engine. All-synchronized 4-speed floor shift, competition suspension with staggered rear shocks, 6-inch rims, belted wide-tread white sidewall F70-14s, exposed hood lock pins and faired side mirrors ... a complete package, ready to go at only $3164—2-Door Sports-Roof (2-door notchback — $25.00 additional).* 1969 Cobra Hardtop with 428 CID 4V Cobra Jet Ram-Air V-8 and F70 x 14 wide-oval belted tires (as illustrated)—$3335.49.*

Torino GT—puts a lot of class in the quarter mile.

The new 1969 Torino GT SportsRoof, Hardtop and Convertible are designed to cut the big time mustard. Just like the specially modified Torinos that racked up all those points to win the 1968 NASCAR Manufacturer's Championship. The difference is, we've cooled them down for street use and added enough style and comfort to make them America's plushest performance cars. The standard equipment list starts with Ford's strong, lightweight 302 cube 2V V-8, adds GT handling suspension, air scoop, styled steel wheels, belted wide-oval white sidewall tires, plus stripes and special identification. All these standard goodies come in at $2823—2-Door SportsRoof (2-Door Hardtop—$25.00 additional; 2-Door Convertible —$250.00 additional).*

1969 Torino GT SportsRoof

P3

Every Ford can be a winner with Ford performance parts

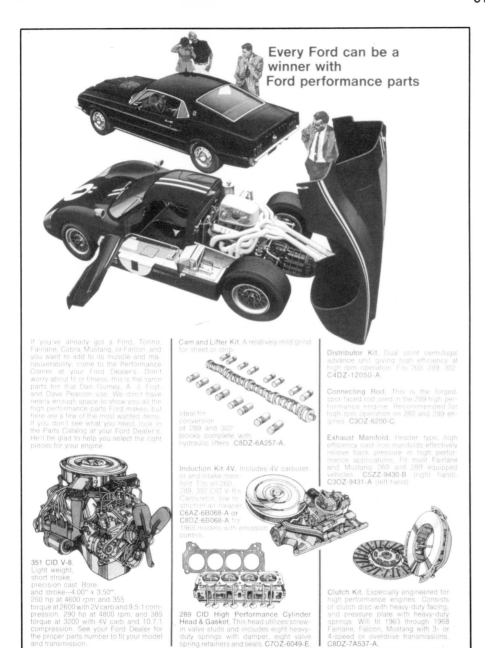

If you've already got a Ford, Torino, Fairlane, Cobra, Mustang, or Falcon, and you want to add to its muscle and maneuverability, come to the Performance Corner at your Ford Dealer's. Don't worry about fit or fitness; this is the same parts bin that Dan Gurney, A. J. Foyt, and Dave Pearson use. We don't have nearly enough space to show you all the high performance parts Ford makes, but here are a few of the most wanted items. If you don't see what you need, look in the Parts Catalog at your Ford Dealer's. He'll be glad to help you select the right pieces for your engine.

351 CID V-8. Light weight, short stroke, precision cast. Bore and stroke—4.00" x 3.50". 250 hp at 4600 rpm and 355 torque at 2600 with 2V carb and 9.5:1 compression. 290 hp at 4800 rpm, and 385 torque at 3200 with 4V carb and 10.7:1 compression. See your Ford Dealer for the proper parts number to fit your model and transmission.

Cam and Lifter Kit. A relatively mild grind for street or strip.

Ideal for conversion of 289 and 302 blocks, complete with hydraulic lifters. C8DZ-6A257-A.

Induction Kit 4V. Includes 4V carburetor and intake manifold. Fits all 260, 289, 302 CID V-8's. Carburetor, low restriction air cleaner. C6AZ-6B068-A or C8DZ-6B068-A for 1968 models with emission control.

289 CID High Performance Cylinder Head & Gasket. This head utilizes screw-in valve studs and includes eight heavy-duty springs with damper, eight valve spring retainers and seals. C7OZ-6049-E.

Distributor Kit. Dual point centrifugal advance unit giving high efficiency at high rpm operation. Fits 260, 289, 302. C4DZ-12050-A.

Connecting Rod. This is the forged, spot-faced rod used in the 289 high performance engine. Recommended for high rpm operation on 260 and 289 engines. C3OZ-6200-C.

Exhaust Manifold. Header type, high efficiency cast iron manifolds effectively relieve back pressure in high performance applications. Fit most Fairlane and Mustang 260 and 289 equipped vehicles. C5ZZ-9430-B (right hand), C3OZ-9431-A (left hand).

Clutch Kit. Especially engineered for high performance engines. Consists of clutch disc with heavy-duty facing, and pressure plate with heavy-duty springs. Will fit 1963 through 1968 Fairlane, Falcon, Mustang with 3- or 4-speed or overdrive transmissions. C8DZ-7A537-A.

POWER BY Ford

Sitting still . . . it looks invincible

Turn it on and let it out and you'll see how that long, low, racy styling dares anything else to come close. When racing expert Carroll Shelby designs a car this way you don't expect him to build very many. He doesn't.

The Shelby GT isn't a car you buy simply because it's handsome and rare. You buy it, of course, to drive it.

Let out the famous ram air 428 Cobra Jet engine in the GT 500, and suddenly you'll know the meaning of the word "power". Wind up the 351 ram air V-8 in the GT 350, and you'll capture the true feeling and excitement of Shelby motion.

Take a corner at speed . . . stab the brakes, and feel how the car is slowed with the force of 11.3" power assisted front disc brakes. Ride through a curve . . . Heavy duty adjustable shock absorbers with competition type springs will keep the fat Polyglass belted tires in firm contact with the road thru all its bumps and dips. A heavy duty front stabilizer bar keeps the body tight and level against the force of cornering.

That's race car handling . . . It's something built into every Shelby GT.

And it's available now at your local Shelby Ford Performance Center.

Shelby GT 350/500 SHELBY COBRA

GRAND SLAM!
Torino wins 1968 NASCAR, USAC and ARCA championships.

And Cobra's coming on for more!

Torino started strong by taking the first five places in the first race it entered, the 1968 Riverside 500. Torino finished strong, too. Specially modified Torinos won all three stock car racing crowns. Boss drivers Dave Pearson, A. J. Foyt and Benny Parsons did a lot of hard charging to get us there.

What's all this got to do with you and our new street machine? Plenty. Something as quick and mean as Cobra doesn't happen until you do a batch of triple-crown-winning Torinos. Cars that go fast grow slowly! With Better Ideas born in the heat and hustle of stock car racing.

Take a good look at Cobra by Ford. Standard 428 CID 4-barrel V-8 rated conservatively at 335 horses. (The largest standard engine in any car in its class.) Competition suspension with staggered rear shocks

to soak up the 440 lbs-ft of torque that beast above throws out. Wide-tread belted F70 x 14 grabbers mounted on 6-inch rims. Four-on-the-floor, all-synchro box, exposed hood lock pins.

If you really want to get down and dirty about it, put in the 428 CID Cobra Jet V-8 with through-the-hood Ram-Air induction, power front discs and Traction-Lok differential. The only surprise left in your life is the price—very low.

Go to your Ford Dealer's Performance Corner and test-drive a Cobra. Run it up to five grand and you'll know we're telling it like it is.

COBRA **Ford**

Cobra strikes again!

Torino Cobra wins Daytona 500

Three races—three wins. Right on top of a 1-2-3 finish in the Riverside 500 and victory in the ARCA 300, Ford's Torino Cobras take three of the top four places in the Daytona 500, with Lee Roy Yarbrough piloting the winning car. All of the 50 cars that started were specially modified for racing. Only 28 finished. Proof that Torino Cobra can take it.

You get a lot of this same kind of winner-take-all action in the Cobras at your Ford Dealer's Performance Corner. Cobra comes with a standard 4-barrel

428 CID V-8, rated at 335 horsepower. There's a Cobra Jet Ram-Air version available. Transmission is a trigger-quick, fully synchronized 4-speed box. There's a chassis to match, with competition suspension, staggered rear shocks, 6-inch wheel rims, belted wide-tread F70 x 14 white sidewall tires, hood lock pins—the works. Two-Door Sports-Roof or Hardtop models. Try some Cobra action for yourself at your Ford Dealer's Performance Corner. See why Going Ford is the Going Thing!

Ford has a Corner on Performance

February 1—Riverside 500*. Torino Cobras sweep 1st, 2nd and 3rd—Richard Petty sets new record in his first race in a Ford.

February 16—ARCA 300*. Torino Cobra wins with ARCA champion Benny Parsons at the wheel.

February 23—Daytona 500*. Torino Cobras win, taking three of the first four places. Lee Roy Yarbrough drove the winner.

*All cars entered were specially modified for racing.

COBRA

1969 Cobra SportsRoof with 428 CID Cobra Jet Ram-Air V-8

Fire & Refinement

In the Shelby GT for 1969, Carroll Shelby has created a car that blends two entirely different qualities: high-performance and luxury.

Seventeen years of running at the front of the pack, fielding the cars the competition had to match, has put fire into this car. Power comes from your choice of two mind-bending engines: the all new Ram-Air 351 V-8, or the unbelievable 428 Cobra-Jet V-8. No nonsense super wide belted tires hang on to the road under the pressure of a suspension that's the toughest set-up this side of Daytona. There's stirring music to be made with the carefully crafted 4-speed manual or 3-speed automatic. And the power assisted front disc brakes come on like the great hand of gravity.

Altogether it adds up to an uncommon Sports machine.

But the fire is balanced by a rare kind of elegance and refinement. Deep nylon carpeting throughout. Handsome

touches of simulated teakwood. Courtesy lights in the doors. Bright trimmed pedal pads. Plush high-back bucket seats. An array of luxury options that include air conditioning and stereo tape equipment. These are the touches of luxury cars.

Together the fire and the refinement make the Shelby a very special kind of car be it a SportsRoof or Convertible in either the GT 350 or GT 500. A car designed for rapid transit in the utmost comfort and luxury.

See your nearby Shelby Performance Dealer now!

POWER BY Ford

Shelby GT 350/500

Torino Cobra—Striking Power!

PRE-STAGED
STAGED

The '70 Cobra's for real. A new top gun car that puts a lot of muscle in your driveway at a reasonable price. Take this one hunting for trophies at your local strip. We bred it to win. You get big inch power going in. The standard engine is a 360-hp 4V V-8. Want to chop ET's further? Next engine is a 429 CID, 370-hp Cobra 4V option. Playing for keeps? Get the 429 Cobra Jet with ram air—when you wood it, a trap door opens to dump 700 cubic feet of cold air into the 4-barrel and you blow off the whole class.

If you hanker to be King of the Mountain and bring home the biggest trophy of the meet, there's just one way to go—get your Cobra with the new 429 Drag Pack. You get Traction-Lok or No-Spin differentials with 3.91 or 4.30 to 1 ratios respectively, engine oil cooler, impact extruded aluminum pistons, 4-bolt center mains. Boss 429 solid lifter cam with either Cobra or Cobra Jet Ram-Air V-8's. You're geared for go with Ford's beefy, fully synchronized 4-speed with knife-quick Hurst Shifter®, or you can have SelectShift automatic that lets you hold 1st and 2nd until the revs are right.

But if you take trips longer than 1320 feet, fear not, Cobra's set up to hang tight like a road car should. After all, you don't send out National Championship stock car winners year after year without learning how to

Whenever they talk about ET's, that's where you'll see Cobra Ram Air 429's with Drag Packs—winning!

build a car that handles as well as it goes. Competition suspension's the name of our game—and that's another Cobra standard! Ultra high-rate springs, heavy-duty shocks, bigger stabilizer bar and staggered rear shocks to soak up takeoff torque on all 4-speed cars. We nail it all down to the pavement with 7-in. rim wheels and F70-14 wide-tread belted tires with raised white letters.

That's the picture. Cobra—a car that hangs in there to win.

Cobra Power Teams

ENGINE	COMPRESSION RATIO	HORSEPOWER RPM	TORQUE
429 4V V-8	10.5 to 1	360 hp @ 4600 rpm	480 lb
429 4V Cobra V-8	11.3 to 1	370 hp @ 5400 rpm	450 lb
429 4V Cobra Jet Ram-Air V-8	11.3 to 1	370 hp @ 5400 rpm	450 lb

4-speed fully synchronized manual transmission standard. SelectShift automatic optional.

For the full story on all the performance Fords for 1970, visit your Ford Dealer and get our big 16-page 1970 Performance Digest. Or write to:

FORD PERFORMANCE DIGEST, Dept. HR-14, P.O. Box 747, Dearborn, Michigan 48121.

COBRA Ford

Wood it... and blow off the also rans in your class!

Survival of the fittest: Mustang is America's No.1 sporty car again.

Mustang came out ahead of the pack 5 years ago . . . and it's stayed out front ever since. Today, it's still the country's best-selling sporty car. Read the facts that favor Ford.

FACT: Mustang gives you more because it's won more.

Mustang (specially modified) has captured more Trans-Am trophies than anybody else. Set 295 speed and endurance records, too. And the know-how gained in competition has helped us to improve Mustang suspension, carburetion, and to develop new engines like the 351 CID 4V V-8.

FACT: Mustang's variety puts other sporty cars to shame.

Six models, including Mustang Grande, Mustang Mach 1 (shown left), and Boss 302. Three body styles: Hardtop, SportsRoof, and Convertible. Eight engines, from an economical 200 CID Six all the way to a big 428 CID V-8.

FACT: Mustang's equipped with racy standards.

Fully synchronized 3-speed manual transmission, belted bias-ply tires, sporty floor-mounted shift lever, and an all-new grille with 7″ driving lamps.

FACT: Mustang's equipped with luxurious standards.

Every Mustang (even the low-priced 2-door hardtop) gives you highback bucket seats, wall-to-wall carpeting, and vinyl interior trim. For safety, Ford Uni-Lock safety harnesses and a theft-proof locking steering column.

FACT: You can build yourself an extra-sporty Mustang.

With options like a spoiler, rear-window louvered Sports Slats, functional "shaker" hood scoop, "grabber" exterior paint, quick-ratio steering, 4-speed Hurst Shifter, tachometer, and drag pack.

FACT: You can build yourself an extra-classy Mustang.

Choosing from options like a vinyl roof, SelectAire Conditioning, AM-FM stereo radio system, power front disc brakes, and tilt steering wheel.

FACT: It takes more than good looks to stay Number One.

You've got to set trends, make changes, offer more, if you want to stay the best. Only Mustang does it all. And that's a fact.

Ford gives you Better Ideas . . . It's the Going Thing.

For more information about Mustang see your Ford Dealer or write: Mustang catalog, Dept. M1, P.O. Box 1505, Dearborn, Mich. 48121.

MUSTANG *Ford*

'71 Mustang. New Style and Handling from the Trans-Am Winner.

MUSTANG MACH I

Mustang has always meant outstanding roadability and nimble handling. Proof comes from three Trans-Am and two SCCA National Rally Championships.

And 1971 brings you even more Mustang. Wider tread. Lower stance. All-new body-chassis. Super slippery Sports-Roof. New optional 351 Boss HO and 429 CJ-R 4V V-8's with Dual Ram induction. And improved handling that *MOTOR TREND* describes as " . . . a definite tendency to hug the road much tighter in cornering."

Mach I has the pole position. Standard thin-wall 302 V-8, all-synch 3-speed floor shift, low restriction honeycomb grille, sport lamps, tuned competition suspension with high rate springs, shocks and stabilizer bars, E70-14 belted tires, color-keyed spoiler bumper, dual racing mirrors, High Back buckets, more. With options to match.

Go for the action. Test one of the six new Mustang models today at your Ford Dealer's. Find out which of these great road cars is for you.

MUSTANG *Ford*

With our 351-4V you get a piece of Daytona, the Atlanta 500, Donnie Allison, and a wide-open induction system.

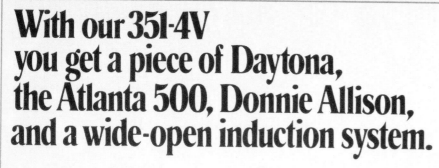

The 351-4V, a free-breathing engine that turns 300 hp at 5400 rpm, is designed for high-speed durability. It provides 380-ft-lbs. of torque at 3400 rpm and a compression ratio of 11.0 to 1. New in the "Power by Ford" lineup, you can order one for your 1970 Montego GT, Torino GT, Cougar or Mustang.

Coupled with a 600 Ford Autolite 4-bbl. carburetor, the 351's "wide-open" induction system breathes better than its competition—even at the mid-range of valve lifts. (Tests certified, July '69.)

351 CID Cylinder Head Port Air Flow Comparison

- Ford 351-4V (2.19 OD Valve)
- Chrysler 340 HO (2.02 OD Valve)
- GM 350 HO (2.02 OD Valve)

Steady State Airflow—CFM at 5" Hg Depression

Valve Lift—Inches
.10 .20 .30 .40 .50 .60

Events like the Atlanta 500 turn up many better ideas. Ideas that make our engines perform better and last longer under heavy loading and high-speed driving.

Every time a driver like Donnie Allison runs a specially prepared and modified Torino, he puts one of our innovations to the test. And a competition-proven idea, like our intake manifold gasketry, is a better idea.

The 351-4V's cylinder block makes provision for 4-bolt main bearing caps in all five positions. Manufacturing facilities allow for growth in displacement in this engine family.

High-speed valve-train stability is assured with the 351's new "positive stop" rocker arms. The fulcrum seat configuration is semi-cylindrical, arm ratio 1.73:1.

The cast iron intake manifold is a new design. It eliminates water outlet and thermostat at the front and permits large runners for an increase in flow capacity.

The specially-prepared and modified Ford-Powered car in the winner's circle at Daytona was virtually a laboratory on wheels. Many better ideas now found in the 351-4V were being tested during 1969's grueling race.

Canted valve heads are not only better for performance, but they permit more water jacket cooling around exhaust valves. The 351's combustion chamber houses 2.19-inch intakes and 1.71 exhausts.

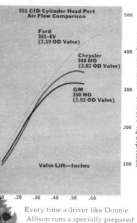

WINNING THE BIG ONES

8/13/69, Dixie 500		L. Yarbrough, Ford
7/26/69, Volunteer 500		D. Pearson, Ford
7/13/69, Trenton 300		D. Pearson, Ford
7/16/69, Dover 300		R. Petty, Ford
7/4/69, Firecracker 400		L. Yarbrough, Ford
6/15/69, Motor State 500		C. Yarborough, Mercury
5/25/69, World 600		L. Yarbrough, Mercury
5/10/69, Rebel 400		L. Yarbrough, Mercury
4/4/69, Virginia 500		R. Petty, Ford
3/30/69, Atlanta 500		C. Yarborough, Mercury
3/9/69, Carolina 500		D. Pearson, Ford
2/20/69, Daytona 500		L. Yarbrough, Ford
2/1/69, Motor Trend 500		R. Petty, Ford

POWER BY Ford

We compete at the track for the same reason we experiment in the laboratory. To develop better ideas to make the "Power by Ford" cars you buy, run stronger and last longer.

Ford

...has a better idea

Special Offer for Ford Motor Company Enthusiasts

A 24½" x 33" poster showing a 351-4V exploded engine assembly. Plus, two "Power by Ford" decals. Send your check or money order for $1.00 payable to:

FORD POSTER
FORD MOTOR COMPANY
P. O. Box 1958
Dearborn, Michigan 48121

Name _____

Address _____

City _____

State _____ Zip Code _____

This offer expires August 31, 1971.   HR-4

Mercury Division

Mercury's new sizzler the...

Marauder

A new breed of scat!

Note the sleek, racy design of Mercury's newest hardtop: the 1963½ Marauder. Aerodynamic styling cuts air resistance, takes full advantage of Mercury's brilliant new V-8's.

No matter which Mercury V-8 engine you choose, you get brilliant performance! A big 390 V-8 is standard on the Marauder hardtop model. On S-55 bucket-seaters, the standard engine is a 4-barrel Super Marauder 390 V-8. Optional engines range up to a 427 V-8.

Marauder transmission choices include multi-drive Merc-O-Matic and 3- and 4-speed fully synchronized manual shifts. Looking for a top performer? See your Mercury dealer.

FACTS ON SUPER MARAUDER 427 V-8: Displacement: 427 cu. in. • 4.23 bore x 3.78 stroke • 425 hp @ 6000 rpm • 480 lb-ft torque @ 3700 rpm • dual 4-barrel carburetors • compression ratio 11.5:1 • mechanical valve lifters • fully synchronized 4-speed stick shift transmission.

COMET • METEOR • MERCURY: PRODUCTS OF *Ford* MOTOR COMPANY • LINCOLN-MERCURY DIVISION
FOR 60 YEARS THE SYMBOL OF DEPENDABLE PRODUCTS

MOTOR TREND: MAY '63. REMEMBER WHEN IT WAS POPULAR TO INTRODUCE HALF-YEAR MODELS LIKE THIS '63½ MARAUDER?

S·55

gets off the beaten track ...in a big way

And how the exciting S-55 gets off the beaten track! Engine choices are Mercury Marauder Super 390 V-8 with 4-barrel carburetor (standard) or Marauder 390 V-8 with 2-barrel carburetor (no-cost option). Or go all the way with dual four-barrel Mercury Marauder Super 427 V-8. Transmission choices at no extra cost include: Multi-Drive Merc-O-Matic or optional 4-speed manual, both floor-mounted. Optional tachometer also available. You can count on it: luxury plus performance in 1963 adds up to the year's most exciting big-car member . . . S-55.

total V-8 power throughout the '63 Mercury line-up

ENGINES	Marauder 390 V-8	Marauder Super 390 V-8	Marauder 427 V-8*	Marauder Super 427 V-8*
Displacement (cu. in.)	390	390	427	427
Carburetor	2-barrel	4-barrel	4-barrel	Dual 4-barrel
Bore and stroke	4.05 x 3.78	4.05 x 3.78	4.23 x 3.78	4.23 x 3.78
Compression ratio	8.9 to 1	10.8 to 1	11.5 to 1	11.5 to 1
Exhaust	Single (Dual for convertible)	Dual	Dual	Dual
Adv. horsepower @ rpm	250 @ 4400	300 @ 4600	410 @ 5600	425 @ 6000

TRANSMISSIONS, REAR AXLE RATIOS

3-Speed Manual	3.50:1 (3.89:1 opt.)	—	—	—
4-Speed Manual	3.50:1 (3.89:1 opt.)	3.50:1 (options)	3.50:1 (options range from 3.00:1 to 4.11:1)	—
Multi-Drive Merc-O-Matic	3.00:1 (3.50:1 opt.)	3.89:1 or 4.11:1	—	—

*Limited production option

Transmissions? **The 4-speed manual,** a sports car favorite with floor-mounted stick shift, is available with all Mercury engines and mandatory with big Marauder 427 engines. It gets maximum performance out of any engine, adapts quickly to versatile driving situations. **Multi-Drive Merc-O-Matic** is available with both Marauder 390 engines. This flexible dual-range automatic transmission provides two forward drives in addition to low, reverse, park and neutral positions. Fully synchronized **3-speed manual** available only with standard Mercury Marauder 390 V-8.

four

Speaking of top performers!

Here are the two performance champions of the year
... available only at your Mercury dealer's

'64 Comet... World's 100,000 Mile Durability Champion

Comet proved its right to this title at Daytona, Fla., by doing what no other car has ever done before. Four '64 Comets—specially equipped and prepared for high-speed driving—each traveled 100,000 miles . . . each averaged over 105 mph, including pit stop time. And the same engineering excellence that made this performance possible is yours in every '64 Comet. We invite you to try this rugged, newly styled, newly engineered car!

'64 Mercury...Proved Performance Champion of the Medium-Price Field

At Pikes Peak . . . at Riverside . . . in open competition in state after state . . . 11 times in 8 months, Mercurys—modified and specially equipped like their competitors—have topped all competing medium-priced cars. Whether you choose the Marauder, with its racy roofline, or Breezeway Design, with its weather-protected rear window, you get the same championship performance. A 390 cu. in. V-8 is standard; up to a 427 cu. in. V-8 optional.

LINCOLN-MERCURY DIVISION [Ford] MOTOR COMPANY

ALL NEW! COMET CYCLONE . . . WITH A HERITAGE 100,000 MILES LONG!

CAPTURES THE SPIRIT OF DAYTONA. Racy, sporty, elegant. That's Cyclone, a just-out model inspired by Comet's incredible Durability Run at Daytona, where 4 specially equipped Comets each clocked 100,000 miles averaging over 105 mph! In every Cyclone: new Super 289 cu. in. V-8, tach, bucket seats, chrome engine fittings, competition-type wheel covers. (The vinyl covered roof is optional.)

COMET A MERCURY PRODUCT
WORLD'S 100,000-MILE DURABILITY CHAMPION

Ride the Magic Skyway

FORD MOTOR COMPANY EXHIBIT
NEW YORK WORLD'S FAIR 1964-1965

LINCOLN-MERCURY DIVISION [Ford] MOTOR COMPANY

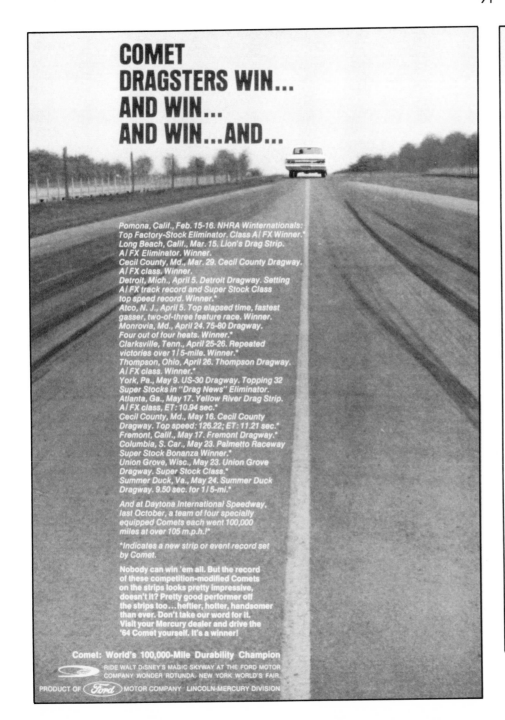

It was cold in February...
except where the Comets were running

Hot results from the tracks

Feb. 12	Daytona—NASCAR Speed Week	A/FX	E. Shartman	Topped 36 SS to win Super Stock Eliminator at times from 10.70 sec. to 10.80 sec.
Feb. 20	Albany, Ga.— U.S. 19 Strip	A/FX	A. Beswick	Took on all comers, won top money with times to 10.88 sec.
Feb. 21	Atlanta, Ga.— Yellow River Strip	A/FX	D. Nicholson	Winner, with ¼-mile times of 10.54 sec. and 10.52 sec.
Feb. 21	Houston, Texas Dragway	B/FX	D. Nash	Ran exhibitions, set new track records: 11.70 sec.

It gets warm when competition-modified Comets wail. Ask the competitors. And you get a warm feeling at your Mercury Comet dealer's, too. Something about the heft of Comet does it. And the solid way it's built. And the pure beauty. And the big things that happen when you sit behind the wheel. So visit your Mercury Comet dealer's showroom. It's a real hot spot.

 Mercury Comet

the world's 100,000-mile Durability Champion

RIDE WALT DISNEY'S MAGIC SKYWAY AT THE FORD MOTOR COMPANY PAVILION, NEW YORK WORLD'S FAIR

Top spine tingler in the Comet line: Cyclone GT convertible.

This one will start a glow in any red-blooded American driver. For getaway, there's a new 390 4-barrel V-8 with a high-lift cam. Quite a start. And console-mounted transmission. (The optional 4-speed manual is specially geared for blazing getaway.) Buckets, of course. And heavy-duty, wide-rim wheels. And high-rate front and rear springs, big-diameter stabilizer bar, and HD shocks front and rear. And twin scoop GT hood. Engine dress-up kit, too. Add the optional tach and you're ready to rally. You get the idea: This Comet omits nothing that could add to the sport of driving. It has a special, spirited luxury, too. In the upholstery, trim, carpeting, everywhere. This new Comet Cyclone GT is also available as a hardtop—one of the thirteen bigger new-generation Comets: sedans, hardtops, convertibles, station wagons...all roomier, livelier and more beautiful than ever. The complete lineup includes sporty Calientes, stylish Capris and rakish Comet 202's, as well as racy Cyclones. Choose your 1966 Comet at your Mercury dealer's now.

the big, beautiful performance champion

 *Mercury* COMET

GT

Introducing Mercury Cyclone '67

Mercury Cyclone with optional GT Performance Group

A man's kind of action from Mercury, the Man's Car!

The Man's Car for men who like their action big! You sense this the moment you take the wheel. It's hefty. Wood-grained. Gives a man that "in charge" feeling. The bucket seats are man-sized. With GT options, this Mercury Cyclone offers every feature a performance man looks for: ■ 4-carb 390 cubic inch V-8 ■ Dual exhausts ■ Heavy-duty running gear—shocks, springs, stabilizer bar, the works! Other options include: ■ fade-resistant power disc brakes and ■ His-and-Her Select-Shift Merc-O-Matic (lets a man run it through the gears, lets his wife leave it in automatic). And, remember, this is the Man's Car with a heritage of performance! Cyclone! Come drive one now!

Mercury
Marquis • Brougham • Park Lane • Montclair • Monterey
Cyclone • Caliente • Capri • Comet 202 • Cool new Cougar

Ford LINCOLN-MERCURY DIVISION

FINISH LINE AT DAYTONA

MERCURY COUGAR

American. (Cougars to be raced will be powered by a specially prepared 289 cubic inch V8 engine.) Following are specifications of the Cougar Group 2 from which the special version derives. Body style: two-door hardtop. Engine: Mercury overhead valve V8. Bore & stroke: 4.00 x 2.84. Displacement: 289 cu. in. Compression ratio: 11.5 to 1. Brake horsepower: 341 at 5800 rpm. Torque: 300 lbs. ft. at 4000 rpm. Carburetors: two 4-barrel. Transmission: 4-speed synchromesh. Suspension: independent coil, front; leaf, rear. Brakes: double caliper vented disc, front; drum, rear. Wheelbase: 111. Overall length: 190.5. Curb weight: 2972 lbs.

Autolite speaks a performance language all its own

And that language is Ford *total* performance. Total performance knowledge requires participation in every phase of racing. So everywhere racing goes—Ford, and only Ford, goes. To Indy, Le Mans, Darlington, Riverside, Daytona, drag strips. And where Ford goes... Autolite goes. Designing, building, and testing new performance techniques. For Indy cars. For cars like the Cougar above. For dragsters. For stockers. For your car, too. Racing is the only road to high-performance know-how. And only Autolite has traveled every inch of it.

AUTOLITE
the spark behind the total performance company

'70 Mercury Cyclone GT. Password for action with the accent on action.

Mercury!
Password for action in the 70's.
Pass the word.

Mercury Cyclone GT. One of three all-new Cyclones for '70. This GT model comes with a unique Cyclone grille flanked by amber Cyclone running lights. Concealed headlamps are standard. So is the sporty hood scoop, high-backed buckets, and the remote control outside mirror.

A 351 cubic-inch 2-barrel V-8 is standard in the Cyclone GT, with options all the way up to a 429 cubic-inch 4-barrel V-8.
For the all-out performance fan, two other Mercury Cyclones are available: an unusually low-priced Cyclone model with the big 429 cubic-inch

V-8 standard. And a competition-ready Mercury Cyclone Spoiler with aerodynamic spoilers front and rear for super-traction, 429 CJ ram air V-8, and a Hurst Shifter.® 1970 Mercury Cyclone, password for action with the accent on action. See the three all-new Cyclones at your Lincoln-Mercury dealer.

MERCURY. PASSWORD FOR ACTION IN THE 70'S.

MERCURY   Ford

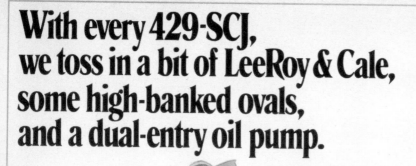

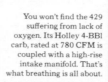

The de Tomaso Pantera. Around $10,000.*

In Italy, men build cars with passion. One of them is Alejandro de Tomaso. And this is his car. Pantera. Conceived without compromise. A car so carefully built (it is virtually handmade) there will only be

2,500 made the first year. Mid-engined like a racing car. An ultra-high-performance sports coupe that stands a little higher than the average man's belt buckle, it seats two (and only two) and it's priced in the neighborhood of $10,000.

Obviously, Pantera is for the few who demand something extraordinary.

The body designed by the world-famous Ghia Studios—is Italian craftsmanship at its highest level. Monocoque construction fuses the steel skin and frame into an incredibly strong and rigid structure.

The engine is a 351 CID, 4-barrel V-8 placed just ahead of the rear axle, which gives Pantera some huge advantages over conventional sports cars. Better vision forward. Less power-loss. Better weight distribution. And the tightest, most satisfying handling characteristics you've ever experienced.

All this is standard: air-conditioning, five forward speeds fully synchronized, independent suspension of all four

wheels, die-cast magnesium wheels, rack and pinion steering, power-boosted disc brakes—even an ingenious system to prevent you from inadvertently selecting the wrong gear while shifting. The de Tomaso Pantera

has to be one of the most impressive vehicles ever offered here at *any* price.

*Based on Manufacturer's suggested retail price. Excludes state and local taxes and destination charges.

Pantéra by de Tomaso [T]
Imported for
Lincoln-Mercury

To locate your
nearest Pantera dealer,
call free, any hour, any day
800-631-1971.
In New Jersey,
800-962-2803.

LINCOLN · MERCURY

Ford

Chapter Four
General Motors

GM Corporate

You didn't think we'd quit while we're ahead, did you?

You don't become General Motors by resting on reputation. Or by producing pretenders. You become General Motors by each year rolling out the kind of sleek excitement you see below. Our driving machines. For '67, they range from the new (Camaro SS 350) to the extraordinary (Corvette 427) and even more inspired editions of GTO, SS 396, 4-4-2 and the new GS-400. If by now you're reaching the happy conclusion that there's something in our GM mark of excellence for you, keep watching. We've a lot more machinery to raise your pulse rate with this year. After all, we wouldn't be General Motors if we let up, right?

Look to the General Motors mark of excellence

Bringing sweet tears to your eyes are (l to r): Pontiac's GTO Convertible, Chevrolet's SS 396 and Camaro SS 350 Convertibles, Buick's GS-400 Sport Coupe, Oldsmobile's 4-4-2 Holiday Coupe and Chevrolet's Corvette 427 Sport Coupe. And the other side of our page will make this side look even

The more you want on a car, the more the mark of excellence means.

Three reasons:
1) We have more kinds of options to choose from. (You know that famous Detroit parts bin everyone talks about? We invented the idea.)
2) We charge less for them. That gets more obvious the more options you tack on.
3) Some of Detroit's most exciting options are available only from us. Like a Ram Air package. A CD ignition. And climatic combustion control.

Of course, what makes our options story particularly fascinating this year are the cars that come with the options.

A straight-off-the-showroom GTO, SS 396, 4-4-2, or GS 400, for instance, is an awfully tough machine to beat. (Just ask our competition.) Heavy-duty underpinnings, warmed and chromed engines, and dozens of engineering improvements are all standard equipment. Yet their base prices are lower than most cars this year.

So whether you're after a car optioned all the way or one just the opposite, our statement still stands.

The more you want on a car . . .

Look to the General Motors mark of excellence

CHEVROLET · PONTIAC · OLDSMOBILE · BUICK · OPEL KADETT · CADILLAC

Before you buy your new car, see what young America is driving.

You probably have some on your block. Young (and young-minded) people who know what kinds of cars are popular now. And what kinds are going to be popular, and why.

Which makes them excellent people to talk to about your new car.

What they'll tell you most about are General Motors cars. Because GM cars are the kind most of them drive.

You can see one of the reasons in the foreground of our picture: the kind of sleek styling that turns heads even when it's not on the move.

And here are more reasons why you'll find GM cars where you find the people you can't kid about cars.

New Engines. Every GM engine is more efficient in 1968. And you can choose from the most varied range of designs in the world... V-8's, overhead-valve sixes and the one and only overhead cam six you'll find in an American automobile.

Sleeker Looks. Many of our most popular models offer you disappearing wind-shield wipers and vent-free windows. Result: another flowing lines.

Improved Handling. You'll enjoy new stabilization designs that provide excellent ride control. And heavy-duty suspension is standard on many GM cars.

Shift Options. Automatic or do-it-yourself... the job gets done smoothly and efficiently in GM cars. The shift console shown above is only one of many you may choose.

Stylish Comfort. All GM cars reveal superb tailoring and careful attention to detail... the kind you'd expect from General Motors' busy Fisher experts.

Chevrolet • Pontiac
Oldsmobile • Buick
Cadillac • Opel Kadett
GMC Truck

The more you look, the more our mark of excellence means.

Our youth movement: Foreground: The Eldorado by Cadillac. Background: Chevrolet's Corvette, Oldsmobile's 4-4-2, Buick's GS 400 and Pontiac's GTO

Buick Division

a great new power mate for the Special's aluminum V-8

Now a V-6! Only Buick has it!

Six for Savings—V for Voom. It was natural that it came from Buick. Natural that Buick developed the successor to the in-line six-cylinder engine...*the V-6!* A V-6 you can now get in the new 1962 Buick Special (in convertible, sedan or station wagon models). A V-6 that has 140 to 179 pounds less weight than in-line sixes of comparable power. A V-6 that gives you the V-smooth, V-lively *Voom* of big cars *plus* gas economy that challenges the compacts. A V-6 with the shortest, most rigid block and crankshaft in any American 6-cylinder car.

Why is it natural that this great engine should come from Buick? Because it was Buick which also developed an *aluminum V-8* which you can also get in the Buick Special. This is the V-8 that gives you sizzling go, yet swept its class in 1961's Mobilgas Economy Run against the country's top drivers. It's natural that it should come from Buick, too, because so many other great automotive advances *have* . . . such as today's safe, simple directional signals . . . fin-cooled aluminum brakes . . . the first no-shift transmission . . . the first hardtop. So here again you have exciting proof that when better automobiles are built, Buick will build them. Buick Motor Division—General Motors Corporation.

'62 Buick Special V6 V8

The happy-medium size

All new! All muscle! All glamour! The exciting '63 Buick WILDCAT! America's only luxury sports car with Advanced Thrust engineering now features three new models—convertible, hardtop, coupe; room for five adults; smart vinyl bucket seat interior; and an almost neurotic urge to get going! Very definitely for the sports-minded male and his equally adventuresome mate. There's a WILDCAT! at your Buick dealer's now—rarin' for someone like you to give it a brisk workout. Why not take time out to do it this weekend?

'63 BUICK WILDCAT

Anatomy of a Buick WILDCAT! Engine: 90° V-8 valve in head. Displacement: 401 cu. in. Maximum h.p. 325 at 4400 rpm. Maximum torque: 445 ft.-lb. at 2800 rpm. Compression: 10.25:1. Bore and stroke: 4.1875 x 3.64. Carburetor: one 4-bbl. downdraft. Valves: hydraulic lifter type. Rear Axle: hypoid semi-floating. Gear ratio: 3.42. Transmission: automatic, torque convertor type. Brakes: 12" Duo-servo. Finned aluminum up front. Advanced Thrust: Re-positions engine forward. Gives straight tracking, flat cornering, easy handling.

Buick Motor Division—General Motors Corporation

Watch closely.
This docile, well-mannered Buick Special will now turn into a fierce, fire-breathing, four-barrelled wonder.

Shazam.

Clever disguise, eh? That beautifully groomed styling, we mean. Who'd ever guess that beneath the Special's handsome skin beats a four-barrelled, 250-hp heart? The Wildcat 355 is an extra-cost option, of course. It develops 355 ft./lbs. of torque at 3000 rpm and 250 horsepower out of 300 cubic inches and 448 pounds. (Make that 418, if you elect our Super Turbine 300 automatic.) Some people like to hook it to our extra cost four-speed, some stick to the standard three-speed. Little matter, really. You'll get your kicks—not to mention crisp cornering and a blissfully smooth ride. You want to try it before you buy it? Why, be our guest at your Buick dealer's. One thing you should remember—especially when you see the price tag: ABOVE ALL, IT'S A BUICK.   BUICK MOTOR DIVISION

BUICK MOTOR DIVISION

The new Riviera Gran Sport or, How we put muscles on the Riviera's muscles

If you start messing around with a fairly normal looking Riviera someday and it suddenly commences making loud noises and leaves you fast sinking astern, that, we're happy to say, was no normal Riviera.

What we've gone and put together is a land version of the wartime Q boat, i.e., a merchantman with hidden guns.

What's this? you say. Buick rattling its sabre and uttering warlike cries? They're supposed to be in the business of making nice, big, reliable, well-engineered, soft-riding automobiles.

We still are. But we've opened a performance branch office.

Which brings us back to the Riviera Gran Sport. It packs what might be termed pretty heavy artillery: 2-4BBL, 425 cubic inches, 360 horsepower and 465 lb-ft of torque. And it plasters all this down on the road via a limited-slip differential with 3.42:1 gearing.

The steering is power assisted, with an extra-quick 15:1 gear ratio available for it. The brakes, also power assisted, are massive 12-inch finned aluminum drums up front, 12-inch finned cast iron on the back. Specify the heavy-duty set of springs, shocks, and stabilizer bar and you have the complete Q boat.

Next month we're doing something mean and hairy with the Skylark. Keep watching this space.

More Riviera Gran Sport Standard Equipment: *Automatic transmission —3-speed torque convertor; 2¼" low-restriction dual exhausts; 8.45 x 15 tires on 6JK rims; bucket seats; console; padded dash; tilting steering wheel; full carpeting; 2-speed wipers; washers; map light; back-up lights; trunk light; smoking sets, front and rear; electric clock; speed warning buzzer; trip mileage indicator; things like that.*

MOTOR TREND: FEBRUARY '65. HIGH-PERFORMANCE LANGUAGE LIKE WARLIKE, HOT BLOODS, HEAVY ARTILLERY IS SURPRISING COMING FROM STATELY BUICK.

**You don't tuck a Wildcat V-8 into just any cage.
New Skylark Gran Sport.**

Stuffing a hulking engine onto a set of wheels is a long way from
making a Skylark Gran Sport. Oh, we have a big-bore engine, all right;
400-cu. in. of Wildcat V-8, to be exact. And it does come on like
gangbusters. But you get a lot more for your Gran Sport money.
A heavy-duty frame, with suspension to match, for instance. The kind
of tough, reliable brakes Buick's been building for years. Steering and
handling that keep the reins in your hands. And a ride that makes you
think you're driving a big limousine, instead of an eager Skylark.
Obviously, Skylark GS is a car designed for fun—and the sort of safety
that lets you enjoy it. So wouldn't you really rather have a Buick?
One of the new Gran Sports from Buick

BUICK MOTOR DIVISION

BUICK MOTOR DIVISION

Superbird.

The Skylark Gran Sport.
400 cu. in. / 325 bhp.
Bucket seats.
Floor-shift, all-synchro 3 speed.
Heavy-duty suspension.
Oversized, 7.75 x 14 tires.
Performance axle ratios.
Zow!
The Buick Skylark
Gran Sport

The Riviera with muscles on its muscles.
New Riviera Gran Sport.

There has always been a vast body of admirers who wouldn't change a hair on the normal Riviera's chest for the world. But we have discovered, lurking in the wings, a cluster of hotbloods who secretly have been yearning for a little more heat. Thus, the Riviera Gran Sport. It packs a 425-cubic inch, 360-hp, V-8 with 465 lb-ft of torque. (Numbers were never lovelier.) And we went behind the firewall, too. A limited-slip differential. Power-assisted brakes and steering. And you can specify the heavy-duty set of springs, shocks and stabilizer bar. What happens when you put everything together is the most exciting automobile to travel any road. Wouldn't you really rather have a Buick?

One of the new Gran Sports from Buick

BUICK MOTOR DIVISION

This is what mountain country looks like to the tuned car.

What makes a car a car is styling, performance, ride and handling. Only when they're all tuned together is the car a Buick. Like this '66 Skylark Gran Sport.

As a matter of fact, it's what miserable traffic looks like to the tuned car. And twisty, winding roads. And a "ROAD UNDER CONSTRUCTION," too.

For the tuned car makes a habit of making unwelcome sights disappear.

Which makes the tuned car a most welcome sight indeed.

The Skylark Gran Sport—one of the tuned cars. The Skylark GS in the picture is, like every tuned car, a beautiful blend of styling, performance, ride and handling. Which means it rides as smoothly as it performs. (A suspension designed specifically for the GS sees to the ride. A 325-hp Wildcat V-8 sees to

the performing.) And it handles as briskly and responsively as you'd expect a car that looks like this to handle.

How the tuned car works its wonders. If you're intent on making mountains evaporate, you've got to get out of the test lab, we say. So we do a lot of our product development out in the real world, on real roads, where real people drive.

All this means you aren't likely to run into a driving situation that we haven't already seen. And *that* means the tuned car is tuned to your kind of driving.

Tuned safety equipment, even. Built and blended into every Buick are padded sun

visors and a padded dash. Two-speed electric wipers and windshield washers. A shatter resistant mirror inside and a rear-view mirror outside. Back-up lights. And seat belts all around, which we exhort you—nay, plead with you—to buckle on. (Is there nothing we won't do to make sure you're in fit shape to come back for more Buicks? Nothing.)

How to turn your country into tuned car country. The only thing standing between you and the tuned car is your Buick dealer. And an easier obstacle to surmount you've never met.

Unless you count mountains.

Wouldn't you really rather have a Buick?

 1966 Buick. The tuned car.

Isn't it about time you stopped playing automobile and started driving the real thing? Buick Riviera GS.

RIVIERA

The extra-strong 425-cubic-incher. Bhp—360 @ 4400. Torque—465 lb-ft @ 2800. Carburetion—2x4 BBL. The standard engine has 340 bhp, the same torque, the same inches, and 1x4 BBL.

Bench and bucket seats are both standard; your choice. Included among the standard safety features are seat belts, front and rear; a second to buckle them could add years to your life.

Super Turbine automatic transmission is standard, as are power steering (with tilting steering wheel) and power brakes.

Chromed-steel wheels are available. A limited-slip differential is standard, with a choice of axle ratios. Red-line or whitewall tires are both standard; your choice.

Heavy-duty springs and shocks are standard. An extra-quick, 15:1 power steering gear is available.

GM

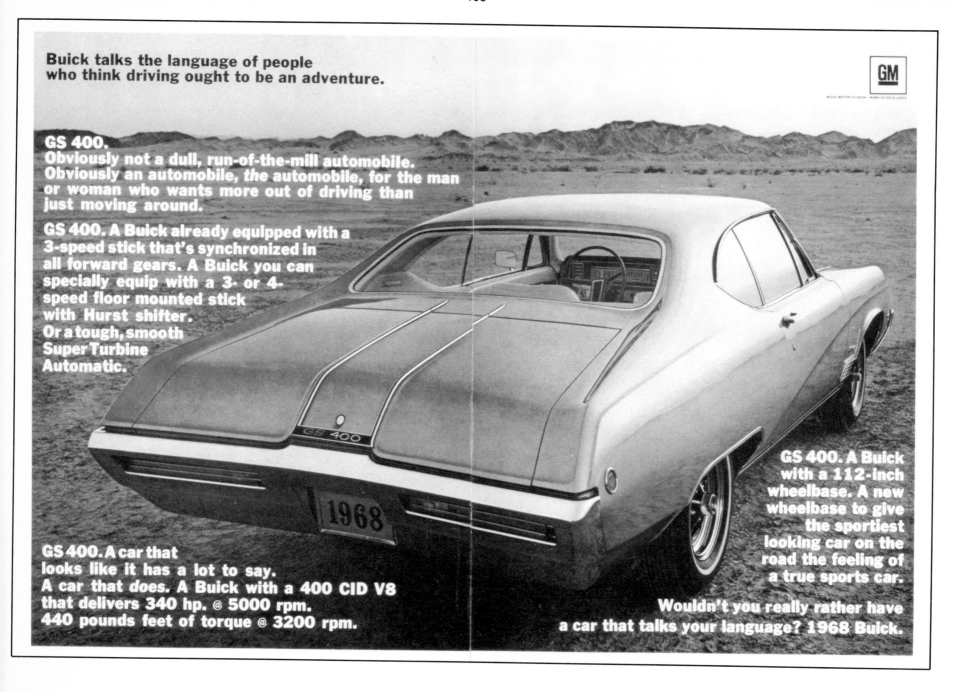

Buick talks the language of people who think driving ought to be an adventure.

GM
BUICK MOTOR DIVISION · MARK OF EXCELLENCE

GS 400.
Obviously not a dull, run-of-the-mill automobile. Obviously an automobile, *the* automobile, for the man or woman who wants more out of driving than just moving around.

GS 400. A Buick already equipped with a 3-speed stick that's synchronized in all forward gears. A Buick you can specially equip with a 3- or 4-speed floor mounted stick with Hurst shifter. Or a tough, smooth Super Turbine Automatic.

GS 400. A car that looks like it has a lot to say. A car that *does*. A Buick with a 400 CID V8 that delivers 340 hp. @ 5000 rpm. 440 pounds feet of torque @ 3200 rpm.

GS 400. A Buick with a 112-inch wheelbase. A new wheelbase to give the sportiest looking car on the road the feeling of a true sports car. Wouldn't you really rather have a car that talks your language? 1968 Buick.

Buick GS-340.
What the car enthusiasts are enthusiastic about.

We started out to build a car that would cost less than our fabled GS-400. We ended up with a very sporting machine in its own right: a 340-cubic-inch V-8, pumping out 260 horsepower. A whole new distinctive look, with hood scoops painted to contrast with the hood, broad striping on the rocker panel, special emblems. Inside, a clean, simple, black interior. And you know what? It still costs less than our fabled GS-400. A lot less.

No wonder the enthusiasts are enthusiastic.

1969 Buick GS 350.

Enthusiasts. Get enthused.

At last, a genuine performance machine that doesn't rattle your molars every time you're stopped at a traffic light. It's the 1969 Buick GS 350.

It's about time that somebody made a car that sits down and dismantles an S turn with ease yet doesn't lumber into a parking spot like a chrome-plated road grader.

Buick figured you were just about ready for a genuine enthusiast's machine. A machine that's good for something other than the Summer Grand Nationals. Like a machine you can drive to work on something less than a tankful of gas.

Get enthused. Over 350 cubic inches of V-8. A 280 horsepower V-8 that delivers 375 foot-pounds of torque and breathes deep and cool through a matched set of functional hood scoops. While a four-barrel quadrajet carburetor supplies the combustibles.

You can add a close ratio floor shift with linkage by Hurst. And a tight yet well-behaved rallye suspension with a front stabilizer bar. And all-vinyl bucket seats.

And confidence that's built right in by GM. With deep, foam padding on the instrument panel, an energy-absorbing steering column and a new ignition, steering and transmission control lock to keep less ethical enthusiasts from taking an impromptu demo drive.

Enthusiast. Get enthused. Take your enthusiasm to your Buick dealer. Then take it right back out with you. With a 1969 Buick GS 350.

Wouldn't you really rather have a Buick?

1969 Buick Stage I.

No wonder Buick owners keep selling Buicks for us.

When Buick builds a premium performance machine, even enthusiasts start talking. Here's what you'll hear.

Stage I begins with a specially modified GS400. Those hood scoops are completely functional. They ram cool, clean air into the carburetor.

The 400 cubic inch engine displacement stays the same. Increased output comes from a high-lift camshaft, a low-restriction dual exhaust system with bigger, 2¼ inch tailpipes and a modified quadrajet four-barrel carburetor with bigger throats.

At the rear wheels, a 3.64 Positraction rear axle.

You can select a specially-calibrated TH-400 automatic trans-mission that provides higher shift points and firmer shift engagement.

And don't forget that the heavy-duty rallye suspension and front power disc brakes are yours for the ordering.

That's Stage I by Buick for 1969. It's a lot to talk about.

It's something else to drive.

Wouldn't you really rather have a Buick?

Light your fire.

Warm up to one of the light-your-fire Buicks, the 1970 Buick GS 455 Stage I.

What is Stage I? It begins with a modified version of Buick's new 455 cubic-inch V8. It gets you a high-lift cam, a big Quadrajet carburetor, a low-restriction dual exhaust system, heavy-duty valve springs and cooling system, even functional hood scoops. It delivers 360 horsepower, 510 foot/pounds of torque.

After more?

You can order an extra heavy-duty Rallye suspension with front and rear track bars. You can add G60x15 super wide ovals, front disc brakes and replace the standard three-speed manual transmission with a specially-calibrated Turbo-Hydramatic or floor-mounted, Hurst-linked four-speed manual.

The 1970 Buick GS 455 Stage I. It's the enthusiast's machine you've been asking us to build.

Consider it built.

Now, wouldn't you really rather have a **Buick.**

Chevrolet Division

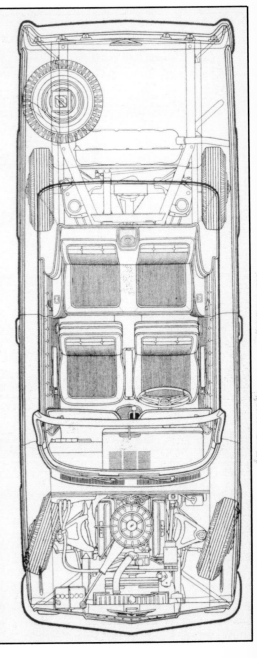

MORE KICKS THAN A SACK FULL OF JACK RABBITS

Some sports cars are good on twisty, winding roads but scream their little hearts out on a turnpike; some pseudo sports cars lap up the turnpike but go limp on a mountain hairpin. The Corvette is neither of these; as a matter of fact, every road in the nation, from one-lane dirt to twelve-lane superhighway, is the eminent domain of this marvelous machine. The Corvette isn't just fun, fun is for kids; the Corvette is pleasure, and we mean in 327-cubic-inch quantities. Nothing else gives as much pleasure because nothing else goes like a Corvette. Nothing else offers that Corvette V8 engine, hooked to the rear wheels with one of the world's finest four-speed transmissions and Positraction (both optional at extra cost), a limited-slip differential that makes coming out of a turn as smooth and simple as pulling out of your driveway. No matter how you use it or what you stack it up against, the Corvette is going to be more kicks, and besides, what would you do with a sack full of jack rabbits? . . . Chevrolet Division of General Motors, Detroit 2, Michigan.

CORVETTE BY CHEVROLET

Chevrolet has all kinds of horsepower for '63!

140 HP

Power plant number one: A new 230-cubic-inch six-cylinder with seven main bearings for smoothness and power that'll make you think you're driving a V8. It's approximately 23% lighter, nearly three inches lower in overall height, and two inches less in overall length. Large bore short stroke design means greater efficiency, too.

195 HP

Power plant number two: Our old friend and yours, the 283-cubic-inch Chevrolet V8, with new cylinder heads and a higher compression ratio for better traffic performance, better highway performance, and better fuel economy in the bargain. And really it is a bargain; it's the workhorse in the line, our most popular engine.

340 HP

Power plant number three:* A brand-new version of the Chevrolet 409, one that can be had with Powerglide.* This new power plant has a moderate cam, hydraulic lifters, a compression ratio of 10 to 1, and a single four-barrel carburetor. It adds new response and flexibility that tailor the 409 to the pace of everyday commuting.

400 HP

Power plant number four:* Basically the same as the 409-cubic-inch V8 that delivered 380 horsepower last year, but now with a new higher lift special camshaft and free-flow manifolding that boosts volumetric efficiency and brings the horsepower up to 400. It has a large four-barrel, solid valve lifters, and automatic fan.

425 HP

Power plant number five:* The King! The most powerful engine in the Chevrolet lineup. It's like the 400-horsepower 409, but it has *two* four-barrels, and bags of torque. It comes with either the three- or the four-speed* stick. It could be described as stimulating. . . . Chevrolet Division of General Motors, Detroit 2, Michigan.

The optional 327 V8's with 250 and 300 horsepower, respectively, are also available, but are unchanged from 1962.

*Optional at extra cost.

MOTOR TREND: JANUARY '63. AN ENDLESS LIST OF ENGINE CHOICES GAVE THE ENTHUSIAST OF THE SIXTIES A LOT OF FUN.

The new Corvette Sting Ray has won the coveted CAR LIFE AWARD FOR ENGINEERING EXCELLENCE

Forgive our lack of modesty here, but we agree one hundred per cent with the editors of CAR LIFE. They think the new three-link independent rear suspension gives the car handling that's far and away the best thing ever to come from Detroit. So do we. They think the performance is on a par with any production sports car ever built. So do we and, we might add, so will you. Unfortunately, not everyone has had a chance to drive one of the new ones yet, because demand has exceeded production, but when your chance comes, you won't believe it! You've never driven a sports car that rides so well, yet handles so beautifully in the bargain. You've never sat in a car that'll turn so many heads and cause so much comment among the less fortunate drivers you pass. This car is a winner! And you'll share CAR LIFE's enthusiasm by the time you've hit forty miles per hour and second gear! . . . Chevrolet Division of General Motors, Detroit 2, Mich.

NEW CORVETTE STING RAY BY CHEVROLET

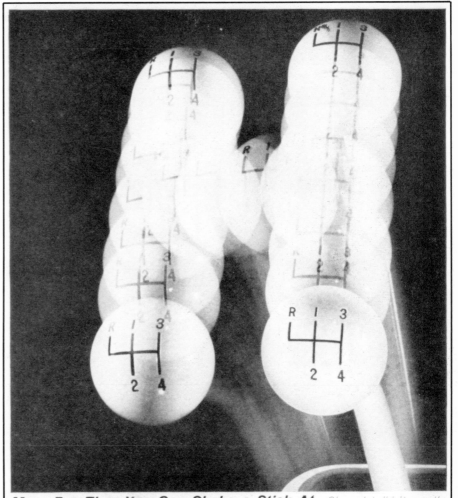

More Fun Than You Can Shake a Stick At—Chevrolet didn't exactly invent the 4-speed transmission, but we have certainly contributed to its popularity, starting with the Corvette back in 1957. Just look at all the people who are equipping their new Jet-smooth Chevrolets with that 4-speed Synchro-Mesh stick shown above. One drive will tell you why. Its crisp, precise response lets you get the most from Chevrolet's superb performance in every driving range, under all road conditions. You upshift and downshift smoothly and easily through every gear like a born virtuoso. Chevrolet 4-speed Synchro-Mesh with five optional V8's and with two low-gear ratios —the 250- and 300-hp Turbo-Fire 327's and 340-hp Turbo-Fire 409 (2.54:1) and the 400- and 425-hp Turbo-Fire 409's (2.20:1 and 2.54:1)—is an extra-cost option. So take your pick. Your Chevrolet dealer is the man to go see.

Chevrolet Division of General Motors, Detroit 2, Michigan.

CHEVROLET
The make more people depend on.

CHEVROLET IMPALA SUPER SPORT CONVERTIBLE

SPIRIT LIFTER

If you'd like to get away from it all, and who wouldn't, this Chevrolet will take you farther, fancier, than anything else we can think of. Take an Impala Convertible like the one shown, or, if a hard top is more to your taste, take an Impala Sport Coupe. Then add the optional-at-extra-cost Super Sport stuff: contoured bucket seats in front, special coil springs at all four wheels, distinctive wheel covers and special SS identification. If this isn't enough to make you want to take tomorrow off, there's more. Additional extra-cost options include a four-speed stick shift or floor-shift Powerglide, heavy-duty shocks for better handling, seat belts for safety, Positraction for better bite, an electric tachometer to help you keep an eye on the standard 195 horsepower V8 or optional V8's from 250 to 300, 340, 400 and up to 425 eager horses. Once your dealer has delivered your Chevy, with goodies on it, you'll never again have to put up with anybody else's wild tales about performance. You'll be driving a Chevrolet, old friend. That's the one they invented the word for!

Chevrolet Division of General Motors, Detroit 2, Michigan

CHEVROLET

The make more people depend on

IS the Spyder's thrust just so much hot air?

A rhetorical question if ever we posed one. Sure, the Corvair Monza Spyder* uses hot exhaust gas to power its turbo-super-charger. Gets 150 hp as a direct result. But hot air alone does not a Spyder make. This is no bolt-on firecracker with a short, loud life-span. We beefed up that 145-cubic-inch air-cooled Corvair power plant to take the extra stress in its stride. Added super-alloy exhaust valves. Redesigned the exhaust valve guides for excep- *tional heat dissipation. And put in a more rugged crankshaft. Then added heavy-duty connecting rods and chrome-plated upper piston rings. Result: performance every bit as reliable as it is potent—and that's plenty. There's something very solid about the Monza Spyder—and that isn't hot air....Chevrolet Division of General Motors, Detroit 2, Mich.*

*Spyder equipment and radio as shown optional at extra cost.

CORVAIR SPYDER   **CHEVROLET**

NEW POWER FOR EASIER UPS AND DOWNS! Corvair's strong and silent new engines never quit showing off. They do it in three sizes for '64: the standard Turbo-Air 164 now with 95 hp, the high-performance Turbo-Air 164 now with 110 hp (extra-cost option), and that absolute braggart, the 150-hp Turbocharged Spyder engine. Best way to humor all three is to find yourself some hills and dales, then just relax as Corvair takes 'em at a canter. Unchanged saving habits in all three, too. All of Corvair's famous features—rear-engine traction and handling ease, 4-wheel fully independent suspension, and flat floor for extra roominess—are back again. Extra added attractions include classic styling refinements and new interior design with pleasing details like map pockets in both front doors of Monzas. If you thought Corvairs were fun to drive before, try one of these new ones! . . . Chevrolet Division of General Motors, Detroit, Michigan.

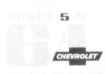

CORVAIR MONZA CONVERTIBLE LEADS A CORVAIR MONZA CLUB COUPE

1964 CORVAIR by CHEVROLET

A 283-CU.-IN. V8 NEVER FOUND A HAPPIER HOME—We slung a big 195-hp 283-cubic-inch V8* into the Chevy II Nova Sport Coupe and now you'd think it was born that way.

This is the same Chevy II that spent a couple of happy years building up a following as one of the most wholesome things since brown bread. The one down-to-earth American car you wouldn't mind bringing home to mother or showing off to your friends. And the last car in the world you'd ever accuse of being pretentious. In short, a regular darb.

Now, with that V8 up front, Chevy II spends most of its time doing impressions of performance types. Give it a 4-speed all-synchro shift* and it's very close to being just that. After all, it started out with certain advantages: taut suspension, trim size, no-nonsense construction.

Is this any way for a nice, quiet, sturdy, sensible, unpretentious car like Chevy II to behave? Strangely enough, yes. Despite its new vigor, it's still a nice, quiet, sturdy, sensible, unpretentious car. With sharper teeth. Grrr. **CHEVY II NOVA**

Chevrolet Division of General Motors, Detroit, Michigan   *Optional at extra cost

Why would such a nice car hang around with the performance crowd?

Nobody said a nice car can't play mean now and then.

Chevelle can get out and move with the best of them—for all its plush carpeting and roominess and obvious love of the good life. See for yourself. Get a Malibu Super Sport, fitted with the 220-hp V8*—the one with dual exhausts, 4-barrel carburetion and such. Makes the most of its 283 cubic inches without kicking up a fuss about it. And gives a Synchro-Mesh 4-speed shift* something it can get its teeth into.

Reacts well to extra-cost options like special front and rear suspension, sintered-metallic brake linings, Positraction rear axle and electric tachometer, too. So will you. In fact, if this doesn't do for your driving what red capes do for bulls, our name isn't Chevrolet Division of General Motors, Detroit, Michigan.

CHEVELLE! by _CHEVROLET_

*Optional at extra cost

Corvair Corsa Sport Coupe

If we tried showing its new performance,
this would be a blur.
'65 CORVAIR by Chevrolet

And we'd never be able to show you here how it climbs, corners, cruises or parks. So here's what to do . . .

Your career as a performance expert starts when you walk into your Chevrolet dealer's and make straight for a Corvair Corsa, Monza or 500 model.

And after one slow circuit around the car you start thinking about driving gloves and Roman villas and such. By the time you've stared at all those businesslike instruments and taken it out for one quick circuit around the block, you're totally smitten.

You think, no wonder they took the time to give Corvair a sports-car-type fully independent suspension. And no wonder they nestled the engine in back. Corvair makes the most of light steering, jackrabbit handling and rear-engine traction.

And you'll find you have a wide range of air-cooled engines to select from that allows you to make beautiful music with this kind of car.

So does the 4-Speed fully synchronized transmission you can specify to go with it.

A few final details—like an AM-FM radio, telescopic steering column, Positraction and simulated wire wheel covers, yours for the ordering—and you're a full-fledged performance expert. Have fun—and don't forget your driving gloves! . . . Chevrolet Division of General Motors, Detroit, Michigan.

Try this on the old psyche

Try a Corvette Sting Ray. Then try to imagine getting out of the wrong side of bed in the morning.

What you'll do is, you'll go drive it. At the drop of a hat, for any excuse, any time, on any errand. For fun. For pleasure. For practical purposes, too—how else can you light your days, clean the cobwebs out of your head, and go about your business at the same time?

If you're thinking about a car like this, why not get the real thing? There's nothing mystical about it. It's pure sports car, all right, but you don't need string-backed driving gloves and a funny hat to enjoy it. Drive it

like it was any old car, and you suddenly come off skillful. That's what refinement does for an automobile. Drive it a little harder, and you begin to see what an automobile can do.

Particularly when it's got the response of a true sports car (starting at 250 hp or you can order up to 375 hp). And the greatest brakes imaginable (4-wheel disc brakes are standard equipment). And the most advanced chassis in the business, for super-stable balance and handling.

Check the price, too. The Corvette is much less expensive than most high performance sports cars.

You can get your Corvette in elegant Sport Coupe or Convertible. And you can order it with anything from air conditioning to power windows. Matter of fact, you can get any kind of Corvette you want except a dull one.

It won't make the grass any greener, but it does color the sunsets a little.

Corvette Sting Ray Convertible

Chevrolet Division of General Motors, Detroit, Michigan

Corvair Monza Convertible

Ever see a guy enter a bend talking European and come out speaking American? CORVAIR by Chevrolet

Fashions change. It used to be all the rage to sit around wishing American cars would catch up to those sophisticated Europeans, particularly when it came to handling.

Meet a sophisticated American.

Corvair has true four-wheel independent suspension, patterned closely after the Corvette (the car that *started* showing people that American cars can handle). A refined front suspension, new rear suspension, wider track, sharper steering, a

little more sting in the tail if you order it, and you get the kind of handling that is currently sending the automotive editors into ecstasy.

Add to that the wide range of other performance equipment you can order for the car—from heavy-duty battery to 180-hp Turbo-charged engine (Corsa only)—and you get a new breed of performance vehicle. Designed to make all those Italians, Germans, Frenchmen, and Britishers turn green with envy.

We can see it all now: you get a bunch of Europeans sitting around the old espresso machine, and sooner or later they're going to start wishing their cars would catch up with the Americans. C'est la guerre. . . .

Chevrolet Division of General Motors, Detroit, Michigan

'66 CHEVELLE

It's different inside and out, as you can see.
And this Chevelle's the newest of all: Super Sport 396!

Now for 1966, Chevelle Super Sport is all this: new 325-hp Turbo-Jet V8, special suspension, fully synchronized 3-speed with floor-mounted shifter, special hood and emblems, red stripe tires—packaged as sport coupe or convertible. Or you can order 360 hp in an SS 396.

Of course, there's still a Turbo-Fire V8 or a thrifty Six for anyone who mostly likes the look and luxury and comfort Chevelle ladles out in 10 other models. New styling, headlights to taillamps. All-new interiors. A jaunty new roof line for the coupes. A handsome new 4-door hardtop: the Malibu Sport Sedan.

What we haven't changed is Chevelle's Full Coil-springed ride. Its stretchout roominess. Its middle-sized handling ease. You'll see, Chevelle for 1966 goes more beautifully than ever between Chevrolet and Chevy II.

CHEVROLET

CHEVELLE · SS · Super Sport

Chevelle Super Sport 396 Coupe with Strato-bucket seats and console you can order—See lots more

Handsome devil

What makes Chevrolet handsome?

Long, low Body by Fisher.

Magic-Mirror acrylic lacquer finish so deep looking it seems you can stick your finger into it.

Smart wraparound taillights.

Rich color-keyed interiors.

What makes Chevrolet devilish?

The Turbo-Jet V8 engine you can add.

It breathes like no other engine.

It delivers more useable power whenever you need it.

On Impala it comes with 325, 390 or 425 horsepower.

It's the most devilishly clever V8 Chevrolet has ever made.

You get it at your Chevrolet dealer's.

Impala Sport Coupe with eight new standard safety features, including outside rearview mirror. Use it always before passing.

'66 Impala – Powered the Chevrolet Way

The big news isn't the gauges . . . it's what the gauges connect to!

The real news about Impala is the 427-cu.-in. Turbo-Jet V8 you can put on the other side of the fire-wall to make the needles quiver. The street version generates 390 hp and 415 lbs.-ft. of torque on hydraulic lifters. A special-pur-pose edition turns out 425 hp and the same amount of torque on solid (ah, what sounds!) lifters.

Both engines are of the same unique design that inspired our successful Turbo-Jet 396, which is now rated at 325 hp. Intake and exhaust ports feed directly to the combustion chambers with little interference from valves and push-rods. As a result, the Turbo-Jets breathe in a manner that makes ordinary engines feel short-winded — even downright asthmatic.

As for the gauges — they're im-portant, too. In fact, we're con-fident that the man who knows what's happening inside the en-gine compartment is a safer, more alert driver. Drive as only you know how — and who knows? — maybe the less knowledgeable drivers will get the message.

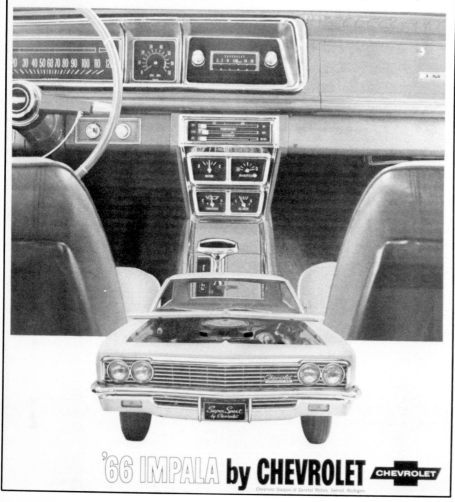

'66 IMPALA by CHEVROLET

Chevrolet Division of General Motors, Detroit, Michigan.

St. Louis, and another spirited event. Corvette for 1967.

The Arch. A salute to yesterday. A promise for tomorrow. So is another spirit of St. Louis, where it's built—Corvette for 1967.

Still America's only true production sports car, the '67 Corvette offers performance from V8s up to 427 cubic inches and triple two-barrel carburetion you can order. Handling from independent rear suspension and four-wheel disc brakes. Comfort with add-ons like air conditioning and power assists. New standard safety features such as the GM-developed energy-absorbing steering column, shoulder belt anchors, folding seat back latches, four-way hazard warning flasher.

Corvette, magnificently balanced and honed. The spirit of St. Louis revisited.

1967 CORVETTE BY CHEVROLET

Cubes, red lines, ft.-lbs., torque, tach.
An SS 396 will even change
the way you talk.

If you could bottle and sell what a new car like an SS 396 does for a guy, you could retire now. Rich.

You look out over a louver-styled hood. You ride on red stripe tires. You control 396 cubic inches of Turbo-Jet V8 (which is a little like driving a storm).

You can add a 4-speed and Strato-bucket seats with center console, disc brakes up front and Positraction in back. It's quick to turn, quick to shift, quick to do what you tell it to.

It's one of those cars you think about driving when you're not and hardly think about anything else when you are.

You'd like to give it a go? Now you're talking.

CHEVROLET

GM

THE QUICK-SIZE
MANEUVERS LIKE MAGIC
'67 CHEVELLE

Chevrolet warrants <u>all</u> its high-performance engines for 5 years or 50,000 miles.

(Including both our 396s and all four of our 427s)

427-cubic-inch Turbo-Jet

We trust *every* engine we build. That's why we give our high-performance jobs the same 5-year 50,000-mile power train warranty we offer on all our other engines. Here it is:

Chevrolet . . . warrants the power train components specifically described as the cylinder block and head and all internal engine parts, intake manifold, transmission case and all internal parts, torque converter, propeller shaft and universal joints, differential, axle shafts and rear wheel bearings on any such Vehicle, manufactured or supplied by it to be free from defects in material and workmanship under normal use and service for 5 years or until it has been driven for 50,000 miles after such delivery, whichever occurs first.

As an express condition of this warranty, once every 6 months the owner is required to furnish an authorized Chevrolet Dealer evidence that the engine oil, oil filter, carburetor air filter, and positive crankcase ventilator valve (and automatic transmission oil and transmission band if so equipped) have been serviced in accordance with Chevrolet's required maintenance schedule as stated in the applicable Chevrolet Owner Protection Plan booklet, and have the Dealer certify in such booklet (1) that he has received such evidence, and (2) the then current indicated mileage on the odometer.

Chevrolet's obligation under this warranty is limited to repairing or replacing any part or parts which are returned to an authorized Chevrolet Dealer at such Dealer's place of business and which examination shall disclose to Chevrolet's reasonable satisfaction to have been thus defective. The repair or replacement of defective parts under this warranty will be made by such Dealer without charge for parts and labor.

The provisions of this warranty shall not apply to any Vehicle which has been subject to misuse, negligence, alteration or accident, or which shall have been repaired outside of an authorized Chevrolet Dealer's place of business in any way so as, in the reasonable judgment of Chevrolet, to affect adversely its performance and reliability, nor to normal maintenance services (such as engine tune-up, fuel system cleaning, carbon or sludge removal, brake and clutch adjustments and wheel alignment and balancing) and the replacement of service items (such as spark plugs, ignition points, positive crankcase ventilator valves, filters and brake and clutch lining) made in connection with such services, nor to normal deterioration of soft trim and appearance items due to wear and exposure.

This warranty is expressly in lieu of any other warranties, expressed or implied, including any implied warranty of merchantability or fitness for a particular purpose, and of any other obligations or liability on the part of Chevrolet, and Chevrolet neither assumes nor authorizes any other person to assume for it any other liability in connection with such Vehicle.

Enough said.

CHEVROLET   GM
MARK OF EXCELLENCE

Camaro
CHEVROLET
By Chevrolet

Command Performance

You don't drive it; you command it!

Chevrolet's new Camaro is here! It's Corvette excitement with back-seat passenger room, a sporting hustler that's nothing but lean and forceful.

Camaro is your kind of car. It has wide-stance design for flattening corners, slim Strato-bucket seats that hang on comfortably.

your choice of convertible or sport coupe and a big-car engine lineup to quicken your pulse. It starts at a base six with 140 horsepower and goes up through three V8s including an exclusive new 350-cubic-inch power plant.

After that, Camaro is up to you. Choose from a series of packages you can add to

make it exactly your kind of car.

Go the Rally Sport route and dramatically change the appearance of Camaro. Make it a no-nonsense sporting machine with the SS 350 package. Or add both of them and get the best of both worlds.

Then go have one great time!

Top left: Camaro Rally Sport Coupe. Top right: Camaro Sport Coupe. Bottom: Camaro SS 350 Convertible with Rally Sport equipment. All with seat belts front and rear (retractors on front) and shoulder belt anchors.

How commanding do you want to be?

Camaro
- Twin slimline Strato-bucket seats
- Businesslike round white-on-black instruments
- Single-unit headlights in a black grille
- Long, low hood line and a tucked-in tail
- Choice of 15 Magic-Mirror acrylic colors
- Choice of four color-keyed vinyl interiors, all fully carpeted
- Safety features like dual master cylinder brake system and GM-developed energy-absorbing steering column

Camaro Rally Sport
- Electrically operated hideaway headlights in a full-width black grille
- Wider body sill molding to accent the sporting lines
- Special identification emblems on grille, fenders and filler cap
- Bright metal moldings on roof gutter and wheel openings
- Special taillight treatment
- Color-keyed body side accent stripes

Camaro SS 350
- Exclusive 295-horsepower 350-cubic-inch V8
- Special hood with raised louvers
- Unique striping around grille opening
- Red stripe tires on 14" x 6" wheels
- Special SS identification emblems

And you can add
- Special-purpose front and rear suspension
- Fully synchronized 3-speed or 4-speed floor-mounted gearshift or Powerglide automatic with any engine
- Special package of ammeter, temperature, oil pressure and fuel gauges and clock on console, plus tachometer and light for low fuel on instrument panel
- Speed warning unit
- Front disc brakes

SS 427
For the man who'd buy a sports car if it had this much room

CHEVROLET

For one thing, you want a sporting kind of engine. In this case, it's a 385-horsepower 427-cubic-inch Turbo-Jet V8, and it's standard SS 427 equipment. Sometimes, when you're not busy, you just like to sit and listen to it idle.

You like a hood that bulges. After all, you've got quite an engine under there, and you don't mind a bit if people know it. In fact, you like things that are distinctive and you know that by its very markings, the SS 427 stands apart from ordinary automobiles.

You want your car to express you just so. And happily, there's a long list of personalized touches you can add to the SS 427 — items like a new 8-track stereo tape system, front disc brakes, 4 speeds forward. Models include a Sport Coupe or Convertible.

You like to unwind. So you really dig the SS 427's stiffer springs, shocks and front stabilizer bar; you know they make for better cornering. The red stripe tires mounted on the extra-wide rims help, too. All of this is standard, of course.

You're a safety-minded individual. You like the idea of the new GM-developed energy-absorbing steering column on Chevrolets. You appreciate the front seat belt retractors and the folding front seat back latches — all standard.

You especially appreciate a dual master cylinder brake system — with a warning light to advise you of a pressure imbalance in either part of the system. You're glad that all other '67 Chevrolets carry the system, too, along with corrosion-resistant brake lines.

New Chevrolet SS 427 Sport Coupe (Convertible, too) now performing at your Chevrolet dealer's.

Everything new that could happen...*happened* in styling, safety, performance

'67 CHEVROLET

Sharp as a tach

You're only scratching the surface until you dig into El Camino's bag of goodies. Dig these: electric tach, speed warning device, Positraction rear axle, Strato-bucket seats (without the console if you like), Mag-styled wheel covers and thick pile carpeting. And put your finger on these: air conditioning, walnut-grained steering wheel, power windows. To top it all off: a snappy vinyl roof. And that still doesn't cover half of what you can order. El Camino's got you covered on power too. Work from two Sixes and five V8's up to 350 horses. Get the message across with one of five manual and two automatic transmissions. Get the work out in a roomy half-ton cargo box. El Camino's long list of new and standard safety items is another strong point. Includes the GM-developed energy-absorbing steering column and four-way hazard warning flasher. Flash a look at El Camino at your Chevrolet dealer's. ...Chevrolet Division of General Motors, Detroit, Mich.

El Camino
CHEVROLET

Chevy II much.

Topside, it's a neat little two-door. Underneath, it's all set to move. Beefed-up suspension, wide oval red stripes and one of the greatest V8s you've ever ordered into action. It's a 350-cu.-in. 295-hp affair with 4-barrel carburetion and 2¼" dual exhausts. Nova SS. We call it Chevy II much. You'll second the motion.

Nova SS **CHEVROLET**

Chevelle SS 396 Sport Coupe. There's a convertible, too.

Its vigor remains undiluted by its comforts. (Another reason Chevelle's the most popular car in its field.)

Turbo-Jet 396 V8 (325-hp!) is standard on SS 396, not something you pay more for. An extra "charge" at no extra charge.

Special suspension and red-stripe wide-oval tires put more footprint on the road and hold it there firmly. SS 396 standard items.

4-speed shift is just what you ordered, big and hefty to handle all that torque, smooth shifting with a short, sure throw.

Bucket seats you specify, and you should. They're thickly cushioned, vinyl upholstered, comfortable as you can get and sporty looking besides.

Four-Season Air Conditioning cools or warms as called for, dehumidifies and circulates air as you please. Weather's always good, when you order your own.

Stereo: available as FM multiplex radio (with AM, too) and/or 8-track tape player. Four speakers surround you with sound, pop, Bach or rock.

Quick-sized nimbleness, big-car ride, roominess, good looks, no wonder Chevelle sells so well. See your Chevrolet dealer and try a Chevelle for size.

SS 396

Chevelle **CHEVROLET**

Be smart. Be sure. Buy now at your Chevrolet dealer's.

GM
MARK OF EXCELLENCE

MOTOR TREND: JUNE '68

MOTOR TREND: MAY '69. WHAT A TREAT IT MUST BE TO OWN ONE OF THESE RARE PACE CARS TODAY.

The class bully.

SS 396.

Challenge it.

That's one way to find out what makes the '69 Chevelle SS 396 toughest in its class.

Just check its credentials.

A 396-cubic-inch 325-horsepower V8.

A beefed-up suspension system poised on 7-inch sport wheels and white lettered wide ovals.

If you want to go the whole route, order the 4-speed, the full instrumentation package, the 350-horsepower mill.

Any way you spec it out, the new SS 396 is a hundred and one percent pure car.

Pick one up at your Chevy dealer's as soon as you can.

Then watch the rest of the class step aside.

CHEVROLET

Putting you first, keeps us first.

HOT ROD: OCTOBER '68. CLASS BULLY . . . A BEAUTIFUL WAY TO PUT DOWN THE COMPETITION.

Camaro SS Sport Coupe with Super Scoop hood.

Camaro's New Super Scoop:
It's like frosting on the frosting.

Basic ingredients, Camaro SS. The Hugger: 300-hp 350 V8. Wide oval treads on 14 x 7 wheels. Beefed-up suspension. Power disc brakes. A floor-mounted 3-speed shifter.

Extra topping you can order: A new Super Scoop hood that shoots cooler air to the carburetor for an added dash of dash.

The whole setup works off the accelerator. You step on the gas, it steps up top end power.

There you have it: Super Sport with Super Scoop.

Add you and stir.

CHEVROLET

Putting you first, keeps us first.

Chevelle SS 396

Chevelle SS. A winner in the 1970 *Car and Drivers'* Poll.

When the readers of *Car and Driver* Magazine voted the Chevelle SS 396 and SS 454 the best of their kind, you know they didn't do it on looks alone.

Fact is, Chevelle SS looks even better underneath. In both versions.

SS 396. Four-barrel, 350 hp. Special performance suspension. Power disc brakes up front. F70 x 14 white-lettered tires on 7-wide sport wheels.

SS 454. 360 hp out of a 454 Turbo-Jet V8. Plus everything that goes with the 396. A floor-mounted 4-Speed or the 3-range Turbo Hydra-matic is available with either package.

And you can also order a special Cowl Induction hood for the SS. Just step on the gas to open the scoop and shoot an extra breath of cool air into the intake. (You also get sport stripes and functional hood lock pins when you order CI.)

See your Chevrolet dealer. He'll show you that everything about the Chevelle SS looks good.

Even the price.

Putting you first, keeps us first. **CHEVROLET**

New Camaro.

Now our competitors know how the captain of the Titanic felt.

You're going to find that a lot of Camaro's new appeal lies below the surface.

It begins at the very bottom. With our completely new advanced-design suspension. It's helped make Camaro's already-precise ride even more precise. To let you drive the car. Instead of vice versa. (Everybody knows how to build a suspension. We know how to make it work.)

Front disc brakes are standard on all models. There are six engines available all the way up to the Turbo-Jet 396 V8 with 350 hp. Four transmissions including a special 4-Speed for the Z28. A wide stable tread. The protec-

tion of side-guard beams.

Inside, a new instrument panel. And new seats. Two buckets in front. Deeply contoured. To hold you in place through the tightest maneuvers. And in back, two semi-buckets that do the same for your friends.

And, of course, we haven't even touched on Camaro's sleek new appearance. You've got eyes.

These are just a few of the reasons why our competition is on edge. They've run into something they can't quite handle.

New Camaro. The Super Hugger. Putting you first, keeps us first.

See it, Feb. 26th. At your Chevrolet Sports Dept.

CHEVROLET

Camaro Sport Coupe with Rally Sport equipment.

Chevy simply has more to drive with.

More cars for starters.

When it comes to performance, nobody offers more kinds of cars than we do.

Monte Carlo SS. Chevelle SS. Camaro SS and Z28. Nova SS. And, of course, Corvette—the car that started it all.

Couple the fact that we offer a wide selection of engines, transmissions, axle ratios, suspensions, tires and such for each of these cars, and you can see how much of a choice you really have. For any number of people from two to five.

While most cars just change, these change your driving. You like to feel the road. You like to have superb handling and know it. You like to go around a corner without sliding from door to door. That's what our cars are all about.

Real driving. Just enough of everything. And not too much of anything.

More fun than four barrels of monkeys.

Ten years ago, there were only two ways to drive American cars. Slow and fast. Now there's another one. Fun. You don't have to go out to the nearest stretch of highway to prove to some guy that your foot is heavier than his.

You should try taking a new Camaro SS out on a twisting back road. All by yourself. You won't have to drive it fast to enjoy it. There'll be a feel of the road, precise control and an absence of roll and sway in the corners. That's driving.

And Camaro's big, fat white-lettered tires, 14 x 7-inch wheels and a profile that's got the Europeans a little "shook" won't hurt your image at all.

As a matter of fact, all of our SS models come equipped with 7-inch-wide wheels and white-stripe or white-lettered tires as part of the package.

We think wheels and tires are two of the most important parts as far as the appearance of a performance car goes. After all, it's not only what you do, but how you look doing it that counts.

Breathe a little easier.

For 1971, all Chevrolet engines have been designed to operate efficiently on the new no-lead or low-lead gasolines. Besides the lower exhaust emissions attainable with this engine-fuel combination, there are benefits in longer life for your spark plugs, exhaust system and other engine components. If these no-lead, low-lead gasolines are not available, any leaded regular grade gasoline with a research octane number of 91 or higher may be used.

In addition, our engines have Controlled Combustion System and new Combustion Emission Control valve for improved engine performance and exhaust emission control.

Which all means that our biggest engine, the 425-hp (S.A.E. net hp 325) Corvette Turbo-Jet 454 V8, will run on low-lead, no-lead or regular gas and at the same time greatly reduce the amount of pollutants added to the atmosphere.

Hot spot: The Stabilizer Bar.

The suspensions we put in our SS models come with stabilizer bars. They serve a very simple function. To stabilize the car. Especially around corners. So you won't find yourself listing 20 degrees next time you take a hard left.

Another way we make our cars ride tight is springing. We use a computer to select exactly the right springs for the equipped weight of each individual car. So it won't be too soft. Or too hard.

Ahhh! Air.

In more ways than one. There's the flowing air of Astro Ventilation in Chevelle SS,

Monte Carlo, Camaro and Corvette. Which means a continuous supply of outside air inside the car, even with the windows up.

There's Cowl Induction for the Chevelle SS. Just step on the gas pedal to shoot a swoosh of air into the engine so it can breathe a little easier. Available with SS 454 equipment. (All Chevelle V8 engines except the standard are available with SS equipment for the first time this year.)

Two convertibles to choose from. Chevelle and Corvette.

Four-Season air conditioning available with most power teams.

See? We've got all kinds of ways of giving you the air.

Our protection plan.

We're interested in helping to protect you. And your investment.

If we weren't, we wouldn't have things like built-in head restraints, luggage compartment bulkheads in most models and a list of over 40 standard safety and security features. All to protect you.

We wouldn't have included things like flush-and-dry rocker panels to help prevent rust, protective inner fenders, an anti-theft ignition key warning buzzer and anti-theft steering column lock. All to protect your investment.

We'll brake this to you easy.

We're talking about fade resistant disc brakes. They're standard on the front wheels of Monte Carlo, Chevelle SS, Camaro, Nova SS and Vega.

And on all four wheels on Corvette.

When you drive one of our performance cars, half the fun of going is stopping.

Now use your head. You'll save your neck.

Take our Chevy performance cars as is, and you have some of the best moving machines you'll find anywhere. Add to them some of the extras we offer, like sport mirrors and Positraction, and you can make just about any kind of car you want.

But do us that one favor. Drive as if your life depended on it.

If you don't the law will get you. Or maybe something worse.

GM MARK OF EXCELLENCE

See what we mean by putting you first?

Hightail it.

New special edition El Camino Conquista in the San Gabriel Mountains, Calif.

Chevy El Camino.

Order a 454 V8 and take off.

This truck is something special. You can even specify a responsive 454 V8. The computer-derived suspension system is smooth and quiet. Handling is confident, precise. El Camino lets you move out with authority.

Performance you'd expect from a road car.

El Camino is built on a Chevelle chassis with a specially modified suspension. Result: car-like roadability with up to 1250 lbs. of cargo carrying ability including three passengers. The advantages of a truck, in a car.

Comfort and luxury are priority items.

Luxury comes in three available interior trims, including the sporty SS interior. You can even order new 90-degree swiveling bucket seats to make getting in and out easier. Special instrumentation, including tach. Variable-ratio power steering. Power brake assist. And heavy-duty front and rear suspension.

Air-adjustable rear shocks help level ride and load.

Air shocks allow load-leveling adjustment by filling them with air through a valve located at the rear license plate.

What else gives you all this standard?

- New pillared hardtop design.
- Tough double-wall doors, hood, roof, cargo box and tailgate.
- Perimeter-type frame.
- Coil spring independent front suspension.
- Front disc/rear drum brakes.
- Air-adjustable rear shock absorbers.
- Standard engine 307 V8 with fully synchronized 3-speed transmission.

A lot more that's available.

SS interior and exterior trim
Four-Season air conditioning
Heavy-duty battery
Deluxe seat and shoulder belts
Positraction rear axle
Console
Power door locks
Power brake assist
61-amp. Delcotron generators
Tinted glass
Special instrumentation
Auxiliary lighting
Heavy-duty radiator
AM, AM/FM pushbutton radio

Vinyl roof cover
Swivel Strato-bucket seats
   (Custom El Camino only)
Comfortilt steering wheel
Variable-ratio power steering
Special front and rear suspension
Wheel covers
14" x 7" "TURBINE I" wheels
Turbo Hydra-matic, 4-speed, 4-speed
   close-ratio
350 V8 (2 bbl.), 350 V8 (4 bbl.), 454 V8
Deluxe bumpers
And more.

How El Camino adds a new dimension to your pleasure.

Wheelbase	116"
Overall length	213.2"
Overall width	76.6"
Overall height	53.8"
Cargo box capacity	36 cu. ft.
Cargo box length—floor	81"
Cargo box length	71¼"
Cargo box width—tailgate opening	64"
Width between wheelhouses	45¾"
Box depth	13½"
Wheel type disc	14" x 6"
Wheel (Rim width)	6"
Tires	many available (G78-14B-2s)

Front disc brakes standard.

El Camino features single-piston floating-caliper front disc brakes. Durable and self-adjusting, these brakes provide resistance to fade and recover quickly from water immersion. Rear drum brakes are finned for efficient cooling.

Building a better way to see the U.S.A.

Chevrolet

Camaro from A to Z28.

A SPORT COUPE. This is fundamental Camaro. Its basic philosophy: a 4-person car ought to be able to handle like a 2-person car. Result: a sight to behold, a delight to get ahold of. For stability, we gave it a low center of gravity. For a firm stance, we spread its tread wide. And a forward-mounted steering linkage offers a preciseness of handling you may not have known before. Yet for all the great road car it is, we kept

it reasonably priced. You see, some specialized body builder in Turin, Italy, didn't come up with this concept of a road car. Chevrolet did.

RALLY SPORT.

Everything a Sport Coupe is, and a little more. We gave our designers and stylists a free hand and they gave us an even sportier looking front end. The grille is stark and clean.

Surrounded by a tough resilient housing. Flanked by special parking lights and bumpers. Hidden windshield wipers and other touches wrap up a look distinctly Rally Sport.

TYPE LT.

The LT means Luxury Touring. Not that other Camaros aren't something special inside. The LT just goes another step. To a world of plushness you might have thought possible in a Camaro only if you had a brother-in-law in California who ran a business customizing interiors. The meticulously designed instrument cluster with tach, temperature gage, ammeter and electric clock is faced with attractive simulated wood.

Rich upholstery fabrics and vinyls are available for the choosing. Woodgrain vinyl panels accent door interiors. And your surroundings are hushed with sound deadening in the front, sides, floor and roof. Sure, other cars come this plush. But this is the one that drives like a Camaro.

Z28.

If performance remains the essence of Camaro to you—as it always has to many—here's your car. This one's for people who really care what's up under that long hood. And for those who want something more in terms of handling. The Z28 comes standard with a 350 4-barrel V8, dual exhausts, sport suspension, special 15 x 7 wheels. Positraction, black finish grille and sport mirrors on both sides. Spoilers, almost a Z28 trademark by now, are yours both front

and rear for the ordering. And is the Z nimble? Quick? That's the whole Camaro story.

Chevrolet.
Building a better way to see the U.S.A.

Take a second to buckle up. It could save a lifetime.

New Camaro Type LT.

Camaro Type LT.

Camaro has a ride and a feel you'll appreciate, too. Steel-belted radial tires are available for both the Sport Coupe and Type LT.

Camaro has a new standard 350-cu.-in. V8. And all V8 Camaros have power steering standard. Tachometer, ammeter and temperature gauge are standard with the Camaro Type LT.

Camaro Type LT.

Camaro not only looks quick, sleek and nimble. It is. Camaro gives you comfortable seats for four people. Rich upholstery. New cut-pile carpeting.

Camaro has a very sensible new aluminum bumper system that helps cushion minor impacts. New taillights wrap around for visibility. You've called sporty cars impractical for the last time.

1974 Camaro. The way it looks is the way it goes.

Chevrolet. Building a better way to see the U.S.A.

CORVETTE

One word that's worth a thousand pictures.

America's only true production sports car. Over the past 21 years a lot has been written and said about it. In fact, *Car and Driver* readers have once again voted it "Best All-Around Car." But words can only tell part of the story. You can talk about Corvette's four-wheel independent suspension, four-wheel disc brakes, radials, shifters, gauges and Positraction until you're blue in the face. You can look at Corvette's styling from the outside in and from the inside out until you're green with envy. But to really understand a Vette's appeal, you've simply got to get it on a worthy stretch of road. It'll tell you a lot about yourself.

Chevrolet

Oldsmobile Division

Displacement: 215.
Horsepower: DITTO!

JETFIRE ⚙ *an exclusive from* OLDSMOBILE

In simple arithmetic, one horsepower for every cubic inch displacement! And JETFIRE's got it. For up front is America's first fluid-injected, turbocharged production V-8—the power plant that's blowing up a storm in sports car circles everywhere. Put your foot down and the turbine revs up to 95,000—gives you a 5 psi boost with a whopping 10.25-to-1 compression ratio. More? Absolutely! Cat-quick handling, buckets, sports console . . . all wrapped up in a honey of a hardtop! Get the jump on the sports car crowd. Pilot a JETFIRE today! Oldsmobile Division, General Motors Corporation.

There's "Something Extra" about owning an OLDSMOBILE!

TURBO-ROCKET V-8 ENGINE—Flows when you need it—economy when you don't. Waste exhaust gas turns turbine (A) which drives compressor (B) to boost manifold pressure. Turbo-Rocket Fluid (C) is injected during turbocharging, permits ultra-high compression.

'64 OLDS
WHERE THE ACTION IS!

Flick the stick...
Cutlass does the rest! Take a hair-trigger transmission . . . tie it to 290 horses and you've got action with a capital "A." That's what Cutlass delivers. Its all-new 330-cubic-inch V-8 power plant sports a four-barrel carb and a 10.25-to-1 compression ratio. Take your choice of a three-on-the-floor, fully sychronized four-on-the-floor, or a silken new variable-vane Jetaway transmission (all optional). But the power-room isn't the only place this bucket-seat beauty has been beefed up. Ten more inches in length, three in wheelbase, two in tread width. Extra inches *inside*. In short, Olds has put plenty into the '64 Cutlass. You'll get plenty out of it!

F-85 CUTLASS

OLDSMOBILE DIVISION • GENERAL MOTORS CORPORATION • QUALITY BUILDERS OF THE NINETY-EIGHT, STARFIRE, SUPER 88, DYNAMIC 88, JETSTAR I, JETSTAR 88, F-85

HOT ROD: MARCH '63. THE ALMOST FORGOTTEN FLUID-INJECTED TURBOCHARGED JETFIRE.

MOTOR TREND: NOVEMBER '63

'64 OLDS
WHERE THE ACTION IS!

A can't-wait kind of sports coupe...with a why-wait kind of price! Oldsmobile's new Jetstar I looks like a goer even when it's standing still. But slip into that bucket seat . . . flip the T-stick Hydra-Matic* into "Drive" . . . and that big, ultra high-compression Starfire V-8 Engine charges into action! Big? 394-cubic-inches-big, 345-horsepower-big. And Oldsmobile's exclusive dual chambered exhaust system cuts power-consuming back pressure . . . makes driving Jetstar I a real moving experience. Five minutes behind the wheel will convince you: *Olds is where the action is!* One final clincher. For all its dashing style and flashing performance, Jetstar I carries a most attractive price tag. Your Oldsmobile Quality Dealer will be proud to show you just how attractive it is! *Jetstar I*

Optional at extra cost.

OLDSMOBILE DIVISION · GENERAL MOTORS CORPORATION · QUALITY BUILDERS OF NINETY-EIGHT, STARFIRE, SUPER 88, DYNAMIC 88, JETSTAR I, JETSTAR 88, F-85

OLDSMOBILE JETFIRE ROCKET V-8 TAKES TO THE AIR!

So powerful...so reliable...so lightweight it powered a private airplane with ease!

Oldsmobile chalked up another record in Rocket Engine history when its new 330-cubic-inch Jetfire Rocket V-8 successfully powered a full-size airplane at Capital City Airport, Lansing, Mich., recently.

Another "First" for Olds!

Modified slightly to meet FAA requirements, this lightweight cast iron V-8 — newest Olds Rocket — actually put a plane into flight. In five hours of air tests, the Jetfire Rocket V-8 powered the husky aircraft in an amazing exhibition of performance and built-in reliability, attaining a rate-of-climb of 1,000 feet a minute!

While Olds has no intention of adapting automotive engines to aircraft use, the flight proves the Jetfire Rocket's superiority under the most demanding conditions.

New Engine Powers Jetstar 88s, F-85s

Available in Jetstar 88 and F-85 models (with up to 290 h.p.), the new Jetfire Rocket V-8

promises you the smooth, heads-up performance you expect from an Olds! See your Dealer today for a test-flight in a '64 Oldsmobile!

Test pilot Dick Marsh (right) and "Oz" Nelson, chief mechanic, check Jetfire Rocket V-8 Engine installation before historic flight.

'64 OLDS →
WHERE THE ACTION IS!

OLDSMOBILE DIVISION · GENERAL MOTORS CORPORATION · QUALITY BUILDERS OF NINETY-EIGHT, STARFIRE, SUPER 88, DYNAMIC 88, JETSTAR I, JETSTAR 88, F-85

If you've got the cap...

Olds has the car!

A digger's dream, this 4-4-2! Here storms a lean 'n' mean Rocket V-8 . . . 400 cubes, 345 horses, quad pots. Goodies like twin acoustically tuned, chambered pipes . . . heavy-duty shocks, front and rear stabilizers and 4 coil springs. Result: unique 4-4-2 action and road sense. How many cents? *Lowest priced high-performance car in America designed for everyday driving!* This woolly machine waits for you at your Oldsmobile Dealer's now. *Hurry!*

'65 OLDSMOBILE

Try a Rocket in Action . . .
Look to Olds for the New!

Oldsmobile Division • General Motors Corporation

442

Way-out-front style (with a belt in the back!)

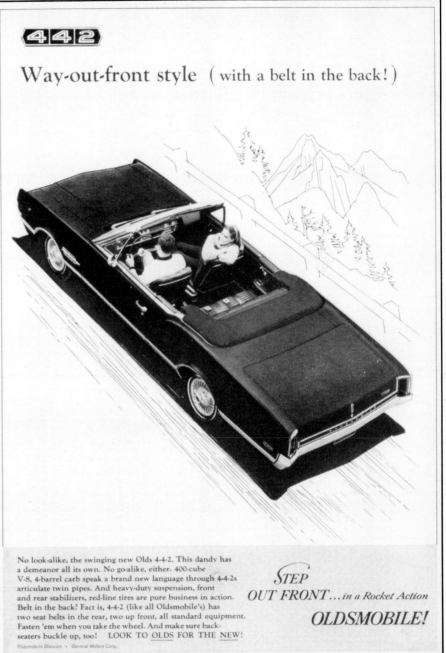

No look-alike, the swinging new Olds 4-4-2. This dandy has a demeanor all its own. No go-alike, either. 400-cube V-8, 4-barrel carb speak a brand new language through 4-4-2s articulate twin pipes. And heavy-duty suspension, front and rear stabilizers, red-line tires are pure business in action. Belt in the back? Fact is, 4-4-2 (like all Oldsmobile's) has two seat belts in the rear, two up front, all standard equipment. Fasten 'em when you take the wheel. And make sure back-seaters buckle up, too! LOOK TO OLDS FOR THE NEW!

Oldsmobile Division • General Motors Corp.

STEP OUT FRONT . . . in a Rocket Action

OLDSMOBILE!

Looking for the lowest-priced high-performance car in America that's designed for everyday driving?

Here's looking at you!

And under that hood, a 400-cube 4-barrel V-8 going for you. Twin pipes *rumbling* for you. Heavy-duty front and rear suspension *working* for you to calm the most cornery, ornery roads. You turn on the action. (Buckle up first — those seat belts, front and rear, are only one of many standard safety features for '66.) 4-4-2 delivers the rest...including a price that makes going the Olds Rocket Action route a real economy move!

STEP OUT FRONT...in a Rocket Action **OLDSMOBILE!**

LOOK TO OLDS FOR THE NEW!

Oldsmobile Division • General Motors Corp.

You'll find enough swingin' things on this page for several good cars.

Or one great one: Olds 4-4-2.

Take a 400-cube V-8 with four-barrel carburetor. Bolt it on a full 115-inch wheelbase. Steady it with heavy-duty suspension and sway bars. Fit it with beefed-up wheels and Red-Lines. Add a high-performance axle for action. Twin pipes for sound. Buckets for comfort. And the cool economics of a modest price tag. That's strictly standard stuff on America's most sweetly complete street machine: The new quality-built Olds 4-4-2! Now let your nearest Olds Dealer show you how neatly the package is wrapped!

OBEY LAWS, DRIVE SAFELY! Olds thinks of your safety, too, with GM-developed energy-absorbing steering column that can compress on severe impact up to its inches; with four-way hazard warning flasher, outside rearview mirror, dual master cylinder brake system, plus many other safety features—all standard on every '67 Oldsmobile.

Engineered for excitement...Toronado-style!
GM **'67 OLDSMOBILE**

highway improvement program.

Project engineer: Olds 4-4-2. Complete with heavy-duty springs and shocks. Beefed-up wheels and shaft. Performance axle. Front *and* *rear* sway bars. White-line or wide-oval, red-line tires. Full 115" wheelbase. They're part and parcel of Oldsmobile's campaign to straighten corners, iron out curves, make flatlands out of hills. Rounding out the package: Nimble 400 CID V-8. Louvered hood. Buckets. Carpets. Dual exhausts. Can be equipped with Rocket Rally Pac, UHV transistorized ignition system, superstock wheels, front disc brakes, vinyl top, and the like. Just pick a road that needs some improving. Then put an Olds 4-4-2 to the test.

4-4-2 One of the Youngmobiles from Oldsmobile

keeper of the cool

Go Youngmobile, 4-4-2-mobile! Equipped to *move* young: 400 CID V-8. Heavy-duty springs and shocks. Sway bars fore *and* aft. High performance axle. Beefed up wheels. All over a full 115-inch wheelbase. Equipped to *look* young: Red- or white-line boots. Pin striping port and starboard. Louvered hood. Bucket seats. Chrome duals behind to advertise four barrels up front. And a pack of standard safety features that just won't quit. For young ideas of your own, choose options like this: Wide oval tires. Rocket Rally Pac. UHV ignition. Superstock wheels. Front disc brakes. (To name just a few!) So what are you waiting for? The youth movement is under way at your Olds Dealer's and 4-4-2 is leading the parade!

4-4-2 One of the Youngmobiles from Oldsmobile

This is the way it is: Olds Cutlass S

Three models: Holiday Coupe (hardtop); Sports Coupe (pillar coupe); Convertible.

ENGINE

Type....................Rocket V-8
Bore x stroke, inches......4.057 x 3.385
Displacement, cubic inches........350
Compression ratio.................9-to-1
Bhp.....................250 at 4400 rpm
Torque, lb.-ft...........355 at 2600 rpm
Carburetion......................2-bbl.
Crankcase capacity......5 qts. inc. filter
  Built-in Combustion Control System provides constant carb air temperature. Also standard: Action-Line 6-cylinder Engine. 250 CID. 155 bhp. 240 lb.-ft. torque. 3.875 bore. 3.53 stroke.
  Optional: Four-barrel-carb Rocket V-8. 350 CID. 310 bhp. 390 lb.-ft. torque. 4.057 bore. 3.385 stroke.

DRIVE TRAIN

Transmission........Fully synchronized, 3-speed column shift
  Optional: 3-on-the-floor with Hurst Shifter, 4-on-the-floor (close- or wide-ratio with Hurst Shifter) or Jetaway Drive.
Rear axle.................Salisbury type, hypoid, semi-floating
Axle ratios, -to-1:.......2.56, 2.78, 3.08 3.23, 3.42, 3.91, 4.33, and 4.66
  Optional: Heavy-duty performance rear axles (H.D. shafts, bearings, differential gears) in two ratios.

CHASSIS and BODY

Suspension........Front: unequal-length A-arms, coil springs, link-type stabilizer. Rear: four-link, coil springs.
  Optional: Rally Sport Suspension (H.D. springs, shocks, front stabilizers).
Steering ratio....................24-to-1
Tires..7.75x14" Blackwall (std.), F70x14" Nylon-Cord Wide-Oval Red-Lines and 205R14" Radial-Ply Whitewalls available.

OTHER OPTIONS

Power front disc brakes. Anti-Spin Differential. Dual exhausts. Simulated-wire wheels. Super Stock Wheels. Rocket Rally Pac. G.T. pinstriping. Sports console. Custom Sport Steering Wheel. Stereo tape player.

GENERAL

Wheelbase......................112"
Overall length................201.6"
Overall width..................76.9"
Overall height.................52.8"
Curb wt. (lb.) Holiday Coupe.....3463
Tread.........front 59.0", rear 59.0"

SAFETY

And all the new GM safety features are standard, including energy-absorbing steering column.

See Your Oldsmobile Dealer

GM MARK OF EXCELLENCE

Young it up. '68 Olds.

Kick up your heels and live a little! Get yourself a new Cutlass S. It has a younger-than-ever look—front, rear, inside and out. A bigger-than-ever 350-cube Rocket V-8 that combines new savvy with new savings. (Or a 250-CID Action-Line 6.) A smoother-than-ever ride, via four-coil springs and improved shock absorbers. And a whole bundle of youthful new goodies—from Rally Sport Suspension to 4-on-the-floor—that let you tailor Cutlass to taste. All three Cutlass S coupes carry the full list of new GM safety items, standard. And all carry very young prices, too.
  Now showing at your Olds Dealer's—along with the full lineup of other '68 youngmobiles from Oldsmobile. So, stop in soon and give Olds young wheels a whirl.

Drive a youngmobile from Oldsmobile   GM MARK OF EXCELLENCE

Toronado: One-of-a-kind car in a carbon-copy world.

If a run-of-the-mill machine is all it takes to light you up, you're in luck. You have hundreds to choose from.

If, on the other hand, you're after something as different and individual as you are, you're looking at it.

Toronado, the FRONT-WHEEL-DRIVE youngmobile from Oldsmobile.

There really is no alternative.

ENGINE

Type	Rocket V-8
Bore x stroke, inches	4.125 x 4.25
Displacement, cubic inches	455
Compression ratio	10.25-to-1
Bhp	375 at 4600 rpm
Torque, lb. ft.	510 at 3000 rpm
Carburetion	4-bbl.

Built-in Combustion Control System provides constant carb air temperature.
Battery .... 75 amp-hr.

Available: Force-Air Induction System. Includes high-output cam, dual exhausts, 400 bhp at 4800 rpm.

DRIVE TRAIN

Transmission .... Turbo Hydra-Matic 3-speed with higher output torque converter, 180° forward power transfer

Available: Floor shift mounted on full-size console.

Differential	Low-friction bevel gears.
Axle ratio	3.08-to-1 standard

CHASSIS

Suspension	Front stabilizer, rear leaf springs, four rear shocks.
Steering ratio	17.5-to-1
Tires	8.85x15"
Brakes	Power, self-energizing, self-adjusting.

OTHER AVAILABILITIES

Power front disc brakes. UHV Transistorized Ignition. Chrome Open-Spider Wheels. Custom Interior. G.T. pinstriping. Bucket seats. Vinyl top. Stereo tape player. Many more.

GENERAL

Wheelbase	119.0"
Overall length	211.4"
Overall width	78.8"
Overall height	52.8"
Curb wt. (lb.)	4472
Tread	front 63.5", rear 63.0"

SAFETY

And all the new GM safety features are standard, including energy-absorbing steering column, seat belts for all passenger positions, many more.

Olds Toronado: The front-wheel-drive youngmobile.

The hidden persuaders:

ENGINE

Type .... Rocket V-8
Bore x stroke, inches .... 3.87 x 4.25
Displacement, cubic inches 400
Compression ratio 10.5-to-1
Bhp .... 350° at 4800 rpm
Torque, lb.-ft. .... 440 at 3200 rpm
Carburetion .... 4-bbl.
Exhausts .... Dual
   Built-in Combustion Control System provides constant carb air temperature.
   Availabilities: Force-Air Induction System. 360 bhp at 5400 rpm. Teams with close-ratio 4-on-the-floor transmission or Turbo Hydra-Matic.
   Cruising package: Includes 400-CID V-8 with 2-bbl. carb, 290 bhp, 9-to-1 compression, Turbo Hydra-Matic, 2.56-to-1 axle.
°325-hp Rocket 400 V-8 with 4-bbl. carb and 10.5-to-1 compression ratio teams with Turbo Hydra-Matic.

DRIVE TRAIN

Transmission .... Fully synchronized, heavy-duty 3-on-the-floor with Hurst Shifter
   Availabilities: 4-on-the-floor (close- or wide-ratio with Hurst Shifter) or Turbo Hydra-Matic floor shift.
Prop shaft .... Heavy-duty
Axle ratios ...... 2.56-to-1 up to 4.66-to-1
   Availabilities: Heavy-duty axles (H.D. shafts, bearings, differential gears). 3 ratios.

CHASSIS

Suspension .... Heavy-duty. Includes heavy-duty springs and shocks, front and rear stabilizers.
Steering ratio 24-to-1
Wheels .... Heavy-duty 14-inch with extra-wide rims
Tires .... F70x14", Nylon-Cord Wide-Oval Red-Lines

OTHER AVAILABILITIES

Power front disc brakes. UHV Transistorized Ignition. Anti-Spin Differential. Rally Stripes. Rally Pac (clock, tach, engine gauges). Sports console. Custom Sport Steering Wheel. Simulated-wire and Super Stock Wheels. Special wheel discs. Others.

GENERAL

Wheelbase .... 112"
Overall length 201.6
Overall width 76.2
Overall height 52.8
Curb wt. (lb.) Holiday Coupe 3628
Tread .... front 59.0", rear 59.0"

SAFETY

All the new GM safety features are standard, including energy-absorbing column, seat belts for all passenger positions.

Three bucket-seat youngmobile models: Holiday Coupe, Sports Coupe, Convertible.
CARS Magazine names Olds 4-4-2 "Top Performance Car of the Year."

Olds 4-4-2

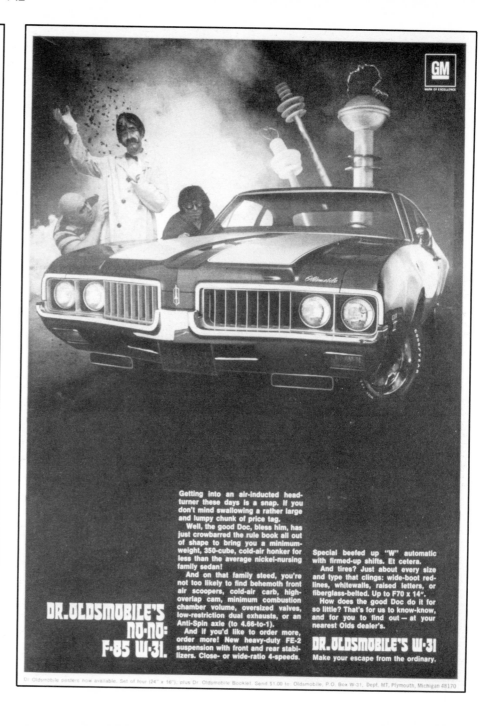

Getting into an air-inducted head-turner these days is a snap. If you don't mind swallowing a rather large and lumpy chunk of price tag.

Well, the good Doc, bless him, has just crowbarred the rule book all out of shape to bring you a minimum-weight, 350-cube, cold-air honker for less than the average nickel-nursing family sedan!

And on that family steed, you're not too likely to find behemoth front air scoopers, cold-air carb, high-overlap cam, minimum combustion chamber volume, oversized valves, low-restriction dual exhausts, or an Anti-Spin axle (to 4.66-to-1).

And if you'd like to order more, order more! New heavy-duty FE-2 suspension with front and rear stabilizers. Close- or wide-ratio 4-speeds.

Special beefed up "W" automatic with firmed-up shifts. Et cetera.

And tires? Just about every size and type that clings: wide-boot redlines, whitewalls, raised letters, or fiberglass-belted. Up to F70 x 14".

How does the good Doc do it for so little? That's for us to know-know, and for you to find out — at your nearest Olds dealer's.

DR. OLDSMOBILE'S NO-NO: F-85 W-31.

DR. OLDSMOBILE'S W-31

Make your escape from the ordinary.

Dr. Oldsmobile posters now available. Set of four (24" x 16"), plus Dr. Oldsmobile Booklet. Send $1.00 to: Oldsmobile, P.O. Box W-31, Dept. MT, Plymouth, Michigan 48170

4-4-2 W-30

There's more than one way to make a car run. You can load up on cubes. Or you can lop off the fat.

For 1970 the good Doc, with the aid of Big Ern (one of his motion-minded engineering side-kicks), accomplished both. They've come up with a new 455-cube V-8 that actually weighs in lighter than last year's 400-cube job! It's big. It's strong. And it's standard—in every 1970 Olds 4-4-2!

Here's how a 455-powered 4-4-2 dresses out when ordered with the good W-Machine stuff . . .

DR. OLDSMOBILE MEETS ELEPHANT ENGINE ERNIE AND INTRODUCES AS LARGE A V-8 AS EVER BOLTED INTO A SPECIAL-PERFORMANCE PRODUCTION AUTOMOBILE!

4-4-2 W-MACHINE SPECS

Engine type	H.C. air-inducted W-30 Rocket V-8
Displacement	455 cu. in.
Bhp	370 at 5200 rpm
Torque, lb.-ft.	500 at 3600 rpm
Bore x stroke, in.	4.125 x 4.250
Compression ratio	10.50-to-1
Combustion chamber volume, min. allowable	91.72 cc
Min. cyl. head vol.	69.75 cc
Min. deck clearance	.002 below
Carburetion	Quadrajet 4-bbl performance-calibrated
Intake manifold	Aluminum
Camshaft duration	328°
Camshaft overlap	108°
Total valve lift	
Intake, exhaust	.475
Valve diameter (Max.)	
Intake	2.077
Exhaust	1.630
Brakes	Manual discs, front. 9.5-inch drums, rear
Transmission	H-d close-ratio 4-speed with Hurst Competition Shifter, or performance-calibrated Turbo Hydra-matic 400, required.
Axle	3.42 Anti-Spin
Exhaust	Full duals
Cooling system	H-d radiator and power-saving clutch fan
Suspension	FE2 Includes h-d springs, shocks, control arms, stabilizers front/rear.
Wheels	H-d 14" with 7" rim
Tires	PK5 G70 x 14" bias-ply, glass-belted blackwalls with raised white letters.
Mirrors	Two sports-styled outside mirrors, left-side w/remote control

Also included in W-30: Lightweight fiberglass hood with functional scoops, big hood stripes, chromed hood tie-downs, and low-restriction air cleaner (W25). "Select fit" of critical engine parts. Reduced body sound deadener. Special paint stripes along body sides. Die-cast W-30 identification on front fenders. Strato Bucket Seats are standard in all 4-4-2 models.

Available: Fiberglass rear deck spoiler (W35). Hurst Dual-Gate Shifter in console (W26). Aluminum axle carrier, cover (W27).

Dr. Olds performance car catalog and W-Machine decal available. Send 25¢ to Oldsmobile, Box W-30, Plymouth, Michigan 48170.

GM MARK OF EXCELLENCE

CAR CRAFT: DECEMBER '69. ELEPHANT ENGINE ERNIE WAS THE MOST POPULAR OF DR. OLDSMOBILE'S SIDE-KICKS.

That gleaming 4-4-2 down there may look like a million. But, in reality, it's rock-solid value.

Here's how we pulled it off.

For 1972, we've come up with a special 4-4-2 Sport/Handling Package you can order on four different Olds Cutlass models. You can get it on the lowest priced Cutlass (Hardtop Coupe shown), two different Cutlass S Coupes, or the Cutlass Supreme Convertible.

And here's what that new 4-4-2 package includes: Olds' outstanding heavy-duty FE2 suspension (the imitators are popping up faster than you can say "me, too") with front and rear stabilizer bars.

Heavy-duty 14 x 7" wheels. Hurst Competition Shifter. Louvered hood. Special 4-4-2 grille. Hood and body paint stripes. Plus exterior 4-4-2 identification. And more.

As for engine availability—that's wide open. A spirited 350-cube, 2-barrel V-8 is standard. But you can order a 350-cube, 4-barrel. Or a 455-cubic-incher with 4 barrels, flared dual exhaust outlets, and a specially sculptured rear bumper. Or order our top package, the W-30 with a dual-intake fiberglass hood and a 455 Cold-Air V-8!

The point is this. Now you can order a low-priced Olds and still wind up with a beautiful performer. 1972 Olds 4-4-2. Go do it.

OLDSMOBILE
ALWAYS A STEP AHEAD

Now there are four ways to get 4·4·2. This is the **lowest** priced way!

GM
MARK OF EXCELLENCE

HOT ROD: OCTOBER '71. THE 4-4-2, FIRST OFFERED IN 1965, WAS NO LONGER A SEPARATE MODEL BY 1972. IT INSTEAD BECAME AN OPTIONAL PACKAGE FOR THE CUTLASS.

Pontiac Division

CONTAGIOUS NEW "CUSTOM" FROM PONTIAC! Coming out of the chute or going in for show, your sharpest entry for '62 is the Grand Prix! From a quarter mile off you can see it's one of a kind. Special grille and rear trim treatment set it apart. There's a minimum of brightwork. And that "channeled" look is real. (The Grand Prix sits a full inch lower.) A long, low whistle describes the interior. Five solid colors. High-wing buckets to make you feel like you belong. The console can take either Hydra-Matic or 4-speed stick shift controls (extra-cost options). (Also holds the standard "tach", so you can watch the engine wind.) Standard "G.P." engine is the fabulous 303 h.p. Trophy V-8 with four barrel carburetor and duals. Cam, lifters and special performance axle to match. There's no match for this one. Get close to a Grand Prix soon at your Pontiac dealer's. Pontiac Motor Division • General Motors Corporation.

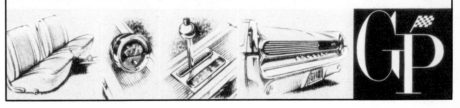

***MOTOR TREND*: DECEMBER '61. THE ORIGINAL GRAND PRIX. BEAUTIFUL THEN, BEAUTIFUL TODAY.**

Catalina: Stormer out of Pontiac

This one comes on with a rush: a new breed of "Cat" from Pontiac. Touch toe to throttle and watch that Trophy V-8 gobble up road. Arc the wheel and feel Pontiac's Wide-Track unbend the curves. Driving a Catalina is a real kick. No question about it. And a good-sized chunk of the fun comes from the things you choose yourself. Engine power: it ranges from a thrifty 215 h.p. rig to the 348 h.p. Tri-Power screamer. Transmission: standard three-speed manual. Optional at extra cost: four-speed, floor mounted stick or Hydra-Matic. You can tailor this baby to your tastes all the way back to the rear axle ratio. And you'll like the basic package, too. The Catalina is slightly longer this year. (Wheelbase has gone up to 120".) The turning circle is tighter for sharper maneuvering. You'll go for its looks, light handling and lightning action. Check with your Pontiac dealer. He's a man after your own heart. And make it soon! Pontiac Motor Division — General Motors Corporation.

TEMPEST LE MANS: DUST-KICKER
BUT SUMPTUOUS

LE MANS   Here's a dude with real authority. It's called LeMans and you can get it as a Coupe or Convertible. The gas-saving 4-cylinder engine is standard. (Horsepowers: 110, 115, 120 or 140.) There's also a special "four" with a 4-barrel carburetor*. It jumps the h.p. to 166. Or you can put in the aluminum V-8* and get 190 horses. Three-speed, floor-mounted stick shift is standard. (You might want the automatic* or the 4-speed manual trans.*) The interior is lush. High-wing buckets, full carpeting, vinyl headlining are part of the package. Get a Tempest LeMans from your Pontiac dealer. It's the sensible (but sumptuous) choice.   *Extra Cost—but priced as low as we can make it!

PONTIAC MOTOR DIVISION • GENERAL MOTORS CORPORATION

PONTIAC'S TEMPEST . . . AMERICA'S ONLY FRONT ENGINE / REAR TRANSMISSION CAR

TRIGGER A NEW TEMPEST LE MANS
FIRE ALL FOUR BARRELS!

There's more to Pontiac's new Tempest LeMans than its bucket seats, comfortable as they are, or its full carpeting and special trim, handsome as they are. The real bomb in this baby lies up under the hood.

The standard four comes in 110, 115, 120 and 140 h.p. versions. But if you're willing to lay out a few dollars more, you can have yourself a four-throated version of Tempest's 194.5 cubic inch mill. This little jewel puts out more torque than any other production four in the world—215 ft.-lbs. at 2800 rpm. Maximum h.p. reads 166 @ 4800—again, more h.p. than any other production four in the world. That's a horsepower jump of 11 over last year. Those eleven horses come from improved carburetion, better velocity and distribution in the intake manifolding and a freer breathing exhaust. It takes premium fuel, and it delivers premium performance.

Next time you've got a few minutes, drop in at your Pontiac dealer's and borrow a new Tempest for an hour. If he doesn't happen to have the four-barrel job handy, either the standard 4 or optional V-8 engine will do fine, just fine. Go find yourself some road and ease open the throttle.

And then see if you can say no to Tempest.

TOTAL TORQUE MULTIPLICATION* WITH TEMPEST POWER TEAMS					
TRANSMISSION GEAR RATIOS	REAR AXLE RATIO CHOICES				
	3.08:1	3.31:1	3.55:1	3.73:1	3.90:1†
3-SPEED MANUAL					
1st—2.94:1	N.A.	9.73:1	10.44:1	10.97:1	11.47:1
2nd—1.68:1	N.A.	5.56:1	5.96:1	6.27:1	6.55:1
3rd—1.00:1	N.A.	3.31:1	3.55:1	3.73:1	3.90:1
Reverse—3.32:1	N.A.	10.99:1	11.79:1	12.38:1	12.95:1
4-SPEED MANUAL					
1st—3.65:1	11.24:1	12.08:1	12.96:1	13.61:1	14.24:1
2nd—2.35:1	7.24:1	7.78:1	8.34:1	8.77:1	9.17:1
3rd—1.44:1	4.44:1	4.77:1	5.11:1	5.37:1	5.62:1
4th—1.00:1	3.08:1	3.31:1	3.55:1	3.73:1	3.90:1
Reverse—3.66:1	11.27:1	12.11:1	12.99:1	13.65:1	14.27:1
TEMPESTORQUE AUTOMATIC					
Low—Plus Converter 3.64:1	11.21:1	12.05:1	12.92:1	13.58:1	14.20:1
Low—Gears Only 1.82:1	5.61:1	6.02:1	6.46:1	6.79:1	7.10:1
Drive—1.00:1	3.08:1	3.31:1	3.55:1	3.73:1	3.90:1
Reverse—1.82:1	5.61:1	6.02:1	6.46:1	6.79:1	7.10:1

*The higher the total torque multiplication figure the faster the engine will be turning at a given road speed and the livelier the performance.
†Must be special-ordered.

PONTIAC MOTOR DIVISION • GENERAL MOTORS CORP.

TEMPEST
BY PONTIAC

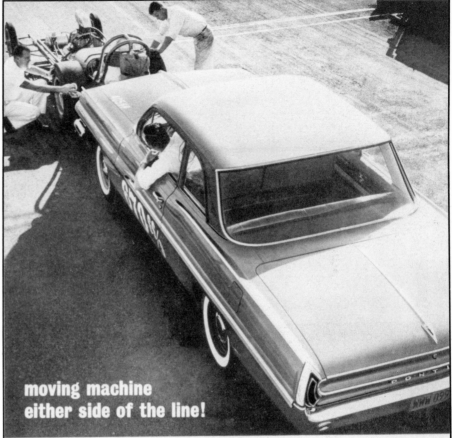

moving machine either side of the line!

Pontiac Catalina

There's a good deal more to driving than a straight-line quarter-mile, and nobody knows that better than the performance-minded. Which is why Pontiac's Catalina shows up so often among you people.

One of the reasons for this popularity is the choice of engine/transmission teams. Standard equipment is a 215-hp Trophy V-8 hooked up to a three-speed stick, of course. But you can get a storming 405-horse engine and heavy-duty four-speed as extra-cost options. And other extra-cost options blanket the area in between, including automatics.

Wide-Track and Pontiac's own special handling precision come standard with the Catalina, naturally. So does a fat helping of pure luxury, without which you shouldn't allow yourself to be.

The great thing is that a new Catalina goes easy on your bankroll—this is Pontiac's lowest-priced full-sized series. Talk it over with your Pontiac dealer first chance you get. Plan to spend some time with him—you could use up a whole day just looking through that list of options, and a happier time you couldn't imagine.

(Oh, and if you'd like to check your Cat against the clocks, feel free. No fair making the Catalina do the pushing while the dragster has all the fun.) Pontiac Motor Division, General Motors Corporation.

"Mind, Hortense, that tabby's got teeth!"

What's mesmerizing Hortense are the four gleaming eyes of a '63 Pontiac Catalina.

Just seeing the car ought to be enough to make you stop reading right here, run on down to your neighborhood Pontiac store, and buy a dozen. But in case you've been away bagging yak in Tibet, or something, and think it's just another good-looking car, we'll bring you up to date. Most of our cars are made for people who have no urge to be the local reincarnation of Oldfield or Nuvolari. But our engineers know that there are a lot of drivers just like themselves, drivers who don't always take the direct route from

A to B. What are fun roads for, anyway?

That's why we make the Catalina such a great car to begin with. And why we make it possible for you to tailor it to the way you like to drive, with extra-cost options like 3- or 4-speed floor shifts (or Hydra-Matic), umpteen degrees of suspension firmness, and 421-cu. in. engines of up to 370 bhp that just can't be fazed.

Go tell your Pontiac dealer how you want your Catalina. But remember, giving a tailored Catalina its head amongst lesser cars can be like using a shotgun on full choke. 'Tain't fair on the quail.

Pontiac Motor Division · General Motors Corporation

Wide-Track Pontiac

Can you tell which Tempest is the tiger?

Easy. The Le Mans on the right gets its power from our 4— that's the big 4 that stalks around acting like a V-8. So you have to call it a tiger.

The other Le Mans Sports Coupe has our new 326-cu. in. V-8 tucked away under the hood—all 260 bhp of it. That's good for *two* tigers. At least. We call it the V-326. It's for people who are willing to admit that our 4 does go around acting like twice life size but still hanker for an heroic V-8. So what's actually with this Two-Tiger V-8 that rates it more than a passing blurb? A weight-to-power ratio of under 12

to 1 that bows only to machines so muscle-bound they can't be driven happily on the street. A whole bunch of no-nonsense torque—352 lb/ft of it. And the only thing smoother drinks kerosene and carries stewardesses.

Suggestion: Take a Le Mans with a Two-Tiger (we've got to stop calling it that or nobody'll remember its real name), order it with $6.24† worth of heavy-duty suspension and one of our no-extra-cost performance axle ratios. Then sit back in that left-hand bucket seat, depress the loud pedal, and blissfully contemplate The Good Life.

Optional at extra cost. †Manufacturer's suggested retail price for specified optional equipment (including reimbursement for Federal excise tax). State and local taxes extra.

Wide-Track Pontiac Tempest

Handling charge—$6²⁴*

Is this ad for people who know all about cars? our Chief Engineer asked. Good. Then tell them about Tempest's suspension. No, not the standard suspension; these guys really _drive_. Fill them in on Group 634. (Ever notice how engineers have a thing about numbers?)

Heavy-duty springs and shocks is what Group 634 is, and a paltry $6.24 is what the whole shebang costs, installed right at the factory.

What it does to a Tempest just plain mortifies those poor souls resigned to wallowing along in their Mushmobiles (a Mushmobile being any non-Tempest laboring under the delusion that curves are for getting flustered in).

Ol' 634 (this number business is catching) is just the start of a long string of low-extra-cost sporting options for Tempest. Like (hold your breath): a tachometer . . . high-output Delcotron a.c. generator . . . aluminum brake drums . . . heavy-duty clutch and linkage packages . . . and oversize tires, to pick at random.

Then there are engines. And what engines! The big 4 of 115, 120 or (with auto. trans. only) 140 bhp—plus, at extra cost, the 166-bhp version of the 4 and the omigosh 326-cu. in. V-8 of no less than 260 bhp. Axle ratios? A no-extra-cost range, all the way from a stump-pulling 3.90:1 to a high-fuel-economy 2.53:1.

Dry your moist, trembling hands and clamp them onto a Tempest steering wheel. You're only young once.

Wide-Track Pontiac Tempest

*Manufacturer's suggested retail price for specified optional equipment installed reimbursement for Federal excise tax. State and local taxes extra. Pontiac Motor Division • General Motors Corp.

*optional at extra cost.   Pontiac Motor Division   General Motors Corporation

Nothing like a quiet Sunday drive to soothe the nerves

Every year we have a passionate love affair with our cars. You'd think it would cool off a bit after we build a few thousand of them. But all it takes to start us twitching all over again is for one of our 326HO* Tempests to go growling by in its businesslike way.

326HO? That's our three-tiger V-8, a no-nonsense piece of sporting goods with an input via four yawning throats,

an outgo via two thrumming pipes, and an outcome that's more than a little startling.

If you intend taking a three-tiger out into the country and letting it out for a gentle, nerve-soothing gallop, we suggest you gird yourself with some of our super-handling stuff*. Like heavy-duty springs and shocks, plus an extra-fast steering ratio of 20 to 1,

for instance.

It's just as well that Tempests come in all of seven different models—coupe and sports coupe, convertible, 4-door sedan, Safari wagon, and the cream of the crop, the Le Mans coupe and convertible.

That way we can keep our love affairs straight.

Wide-Track Pontiac Tempest

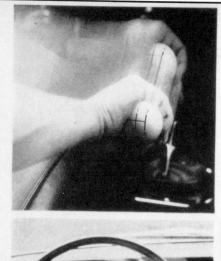

GTO is for kicking up the kind of storm that others just talk up.

Standard Equipment: engine: 389-cu. in. Pontiac with 1-4BBL/ bhp—325 @ 4800; torque—428 lb-ft @ 3200 rpm/dual-exhaust system/3-speed stick with Hurst shifter/heavy-duty clutch/ heavy-duty springs, shocks, stabilizer bar/special 7.50 x 14 red-line high-speed nylon cord tires (rayon cord whitewalls optional at no extra cost)/14 x 6JK wide-rim wheels/high-capacity radiator / declutching fan / high-capacity battery (66 plate, 61 amp. hr.)/chromed air cleaner, rocker covers, oil filler cap/bucket seats/standard axle ratio 3.23:1 (3.08, 3.36*, 3.55* to 1 available on special order at no extra cost). **And some of our extra-cost Performance Options:** engine: 389-cu. in. Pontiac with 3-2BBL (Code #809); bhp—348 @ 4900;

Available only with heavy-duty options at slight additional charge.

torque—428 lb-ft @ 3600; 3.55:1 axle ratio standard with this engine option/4-speed with Hurst shifter (gear ratios 2.56:1, 1.91:1, 1.48:1, 1.00:1, and 2.64:1 reverse)/2-speed automatic with 2.20:1 torque converter/Safe-T-Track limited-slip differential (Code #701)/3.90:1 axle ratio available on special order with metallic brake linings, heavy-duty radiator and Safe-T-Track/handling kit—20:1 quick steering and extra-firm-control heavy-duty shocks (Code #612)/high-performance full transistor (breakerless) ignition (Code #671)/tachometer (Code #452)/custom sports steering wheel (Code #524)/exhaust splitters (Dealer installed)/wire wheel discs (Dealer installed)/ custom wheel discs, with spinner and brake cooling holes (Code #521)/console (Code #601).

the GTO makers—Pontiac
PONTIAC MOTOR DIVISION • GENERAL MOTORS CORPORATION

Get in, turn on,   leave abruptly.

This is where you aim a Catalina *2+2* from. Bucket seats, nylon-blend carpeting, custom steering wheel, the whole bit, all color-coordinated, in either sports coupe or convertible form.

The standard 389-cubic inch engine puts out 283 bhp when coupled to a 4-speed box*, 267 bhp with 3-speed Hydra-Matic*. (The *2+2* comes only with one of these two trans-

missions.) Both shifters are mounted in the standard console. Much automobile.

If you want to make even more automobile of it, there's nothing to stop you from huddling with a Pontiac salesman and a list of performance options and doing wild things with an order form.

Optional at extra cost.

the 2+2 makers—Pontiac
PONTIAC MOTOR DIVISION • GENERAL MOTORS CORPORATION

There's a tiger loose in the streets.

It's late and your bedroom window is open. It's so quiet you can hear the frogs croaking out by the crossroads a good quarter mile away.

After a while a big-engined Something rumbles by in the night. It checks for a moment at the lights, then swings out onto the highway.

Suddenly a rising moan overrides the rumble as a bunch of extra throats get kicked wide open and start vacuuming air by the cubic acre. The moan gets drowned out in its turn by a booming exhaust note that someone ought to bottle and sell as pure essence of Car.

Three times the sound peaks, falls back, peaks again. The last shift into fourth, a throttling back to cruising speed, a dwindling grumble of thunder, and . . . gone. The frogs take up again where they left off.

Have you tried one of our 421s*? *370, 390, or 300 bhp available at extra cost.

the 421 makers—Pontiac

PONTIAC MOTOR DIVISION · GENERAL MOTORS CORPORATION

Pontiac Motor Division · General Motors Corporation

Stop telling me I'm beautiful. Love me for what's inside.

Of course the 2+2 is beautiful. If it was ugly it wouldn't be a Pontiac, right? The real reasons for wanting a 2+2 are unseen mechanical things. But they can be felt, oh boy, can they be felt. (The 421-cu. in. V-8 engine can also be heard occasionally. It makes a very stirring noise.) The 2+2 has a standard equipment 3-speed all-synchro transmission, with a Hurst shifter, lemme-at-em suspension that makes it handle and stick to the road like a little-bitty old sports car, and very secure-feeling bucket seats —all silent, but very impressive. There's a lot of wild optional stuff too. To be honest, we think the insides are as beautiful as the outsides, but then we build it.

Wide-Track Tigers: 2+2/GTO

Pontiac Motor Division · General Motors Corporation

You can get a set of five big full-color action shots of the GTO and 2 + 2—suitable for framing—see details below.

We call it GTO. Purists call it names. You'll call it fantastic.

GTO means *Gran Turismo Omologato*. In Italian, that means about twenty thousand bucks. The way we say it is easier to pronounce and it costs less besides. For a better definition, you have to ask the owners of Pontiac GTOs. They say it means a beautiful car with a swift, smooth 389-cubic inch engine, suspension that makes it handle like our ads say it will, and brakes that stop it right here and now. Why would a car like this make the purists mad? Maybe we should raise the price.

Pontiac will send you a set of five huge 26" x 11½" full-color reproductions of the famous Wide-Track Tigers in action just like the one above—along with a complete set of specs and tune-up tips—and they're suitable for framing. Send 25¢ to cover handling and mailing to Wide-Track Tigers, P. O. Box 888A, 196 Wide-Track Blvd., Pontiac, Michigan.   (No stamps please.)

Quick Wide-Track Tigers—Pontiac GTO and 2 + 2

Our 1966 version of the double whammy.

That heroic time-machine you see on top is the new *Gran Turismo Omologato*, otherwise known as the redoubtable Pontiac GTO or GeeTO Tiger. Under its hood is a 335-hp engine with quad carburetion that delivers torque as if the supply were limitless—431 lb.-ft. at 3200 rpm. There's a 360-hp variation on the same theme with carburetion by the three deuces. Standard box is a 3-speed all-synchro column shift. Heavy-duty 3-speed or four-speed are available, both with Hurst floor shifter. New buckets are practically wraparound. Suspension? Heavy-duty, of course. Options? You name it, we've got it. Probably chromed.

Right underneath the GTO is its illustrious counterpart, the Pontiac 2+2. Its standard 421-cubic inch engine delivers 338 hp and 459 lb.-ft. of torque out of a four barrel. You can specify up to 376 hp with a tri-carb just by marking the right square on the order blank. Like the GTO, air cleaner and rocker covers are chromed, body pinstriped. Inside there are enveloping new buckets, carpeting, an all-synchro 3-speed floor shifter.

And don't forget that we practically invented performance options. For the last word, go to your Pontiac dealer's and wangle the GTO/2+2 catalog. It's in there.

Pontiac Motor Division • General Motors Corporation

CAR LIFE: NOVEMBER '65. DOUBLE WHAMMY IS CORRECT. BOTH OF THESE FACTORY STOCK PONTIACS COULD REACH 95 MPH IN THE QUARTER MILE.

Pontiac Motor Division · General Motors Corporation.

Like our new OHC Six? Get a set of five full-color action shots of it and the other famous Wide-Track Tigers—all suitable for framing. See details below.

GeeTO Tiger, Jr.

The toughest kid on the block now has a mean little brother. Identifying characteristics are stripes on the flanks and an exhaust note just this side of shattering glass. Motive power is that exotic new plumbing, the Pontiac OHC Six. The 10.5-to-1, 207-hp edition that eats air through a Quadrajet 4-BBL and spits

out rpm's by the thousands. Shake a moist hand with our new OHC Sports package. Available on any Tempest or LeMans, except wagons.
The little tiger weighs in at a couple hundred pounds and comparable dollars less than our GTO. (Most of that weight comes off the front end, so you can imagine the delightful repercussions in the handling department.) Sports striping, special emblems, heavy-duty suspension and an all-synchro 3-speed with Hurst

come with the package. Ditto chromed air cleaner, Sunday-dress cam cover and split exhaust manifold. And you can lovingly apply a 4-speed stick, sports steering wheel, slotted rally wheels with red brake drums and all that beauty. (You can forget asking for safety items like front and rear seat belts. They're yours without asking this year.)
It's all written down in the GTO/2+2 family album. Available at your corner Pontiac store.

Pontiac will send you a set of five, ready-to-frame, 26" x 11½" full-color reproductions of the famous GTO, 2+2, and new OHC Six in action just like you see above—plus a full set of factory specs on all three, plus five GTO emblem decals. Send 25¢ (35¢ outside USA) to: Wide-Track Tigers, P.O. Box 888B, 196 Wide-Track Blvd., Pontiac, Mich. 48053. (No stamps please.)

3 Wide-Track Tigers—2+2, GTO and OHC Six

The great impostor.

There's an enormously capable Overhead Cam Six under the hood that delivers 215 hp at 5200 rpm without straining. Special suspension that practically laminates the wheels to the asphalt. A brute of an all-synchro 3-speed mounted on the floor.

Or you can order an all-synchro 4-speed, also floor-mounted. And choose from options like front-wheel disc brakes, hood-mounted tachometer, Rally I or Rally II wheels (shown), fully instrumented Rally Cluster.

The Sprint option is available on all Pontiac Tempests and Le Mans except station wagon models.

Standard safety features include front seat shoulder belt anchors, passenger-guard door locks, a four-way hazard warning flasher, and the energy absorbing steering column developed by General Motors.

If this is an impostor, who needs the real European thing? And you save about $9,000.

Pontiac OHC Sprint / Ride the Wide-Track Winning Streak

After this, you'll never go back to driving whatever you're driving.

If you can stop drooling for a moment, we'd like to tell you what's propelling that Firebird 400 in the picture. What it is, is 400 cubes of chromed V-8. And what it puts out is 325 hp. (Even without our extra-cost Ram Air package, that makes those dual scoops functional.)

The point being, that Pontiac Firebird 400 was designed for heroic driving.

To assist you in this noble venture, the 400 comes with a heavy-duty 3-speed floor shift, extra sticky suspension and a set of duals that announce your coming like the brass section of the New York Philharmonic.

Taken as she comes, Firebird 400 is a lot of machine, but you can order things like a 4-speed (or our stupendous 1-2-3 Turbo Hydra-Matic), mag-type steel wheels, special Koni adjustable shocks and a hood-mounted tach. Naturally, the GM safety package is standard.

Of course, if the 400 is too much car for you, there are four other Firebirds to choose from. Lucky you.

Firebird 400. One of Pontiac's Magnificent Five.

Picture this. We'll send you six 24" x 13½" full-color pictures of Firebird 400, Pontiac 2 + 2, GTO and OHC Sprint, plus complete specs and decals. Send 25¢ (35¢ outside USA) to '67 Wide-Tracks, P.O. Box 880B, 196 Wide-Track Blvd., Pontiac, Mich. 48056. Include your ZIP code.

If you thought Pontiac was coming out with just another sports car, you don't know Pontiac!

Firebird 400

Firebird

Firebird Sprint

Firebird 326

Firebird HO

GM
MARK OF EXCELLENCE

Pontiac announces not one, two, three or four, but five magnificent new Firebirds for every kind of driving.

Now you can choose from five new Firebirds with the same advanced Pontiac styling, but with five entirely different driving personalities. And they all come with supple expanded vinyl interiors, road-gripping wide-oval tires, wood grain styled dash, exclusive space-saver collapsible spare, bucket seats (or you can order bench in coupes) and GM's standard safety package. Which Firebird is for you? Read on.

Firebird

This is our economy Firebird—with the same exciting options and interiors as the more exotic ones. What gives it its unique personality is that it was designed for inexpensive fun driving. Its Overhead Cam Six squeezes 165 hp from regular. Order it with a column-mounted 3-speed or automatic. Like all Firebirds, it comes with seat belts with pushbutton buckles, front and rear.

Firebird Sprint

Now you don't have to go to Europe for a sophisticated road machine. Firebird Sprint's standard motivation is a 215-hp version of our eager Overhead Cam Six. It's mounted on special suspension that practically welds it to the road. (Any road!) It comes with a floor-mounted all-synchro 3-speed and special emblems. And you can order front wheel disc brakes and a hood-mounted tach.

Firebird 326

Is there room for a family in a sports car? There is now. The Firebird 326 combines the excitement of a sports car with the practicality of a 326 cubic inch V-8 that delivers 250 hp on regular gas. (Yes, we said 250!) Standard transmission is an all-synchro three-speed, but you can order an automatic that does all the work for you, and options that include everything from air conditioning to stereo.

Firebird HO

HO stands for High Output. As a split second behind the wheel will attest to. The Firebird HO boasts a 285-hp V-8 with a four-barrel carburetor, dual exhausts and sport striping. Standard stick is a column-mounted three-speed. Or you can specify an all-synchro floor-mounted four-speed or automatic. Naturally, all Firebird options such as Rally wheels and gauge cluster are available.

Firebird 400

After this, there isn't any more. Coiled under those dual scoops is a 400 cubic inch V-8 that shrugs off 325 hp. It's connected to a floor-mounted heavy-duty three-speed. On special suspension with redline wide-oval tires. You can order it with a close- or wide-ratio four-speed. Or with our stupendous three-speed Turbo Hydra-Matic. This could be called the ultimate in grand touring machines. (It will be.)

The Magnificent Five are here!

Leave it to Pontiac to do it right.

Pontiac Motor Division

SPORTS ILLUSTRATED: MARCH 6, 1967. FIREBIRD HAD QUITE A LINEUP, EVEN BEFORE THE FAMOUS TRANS-AM.

Return of The Great One

Pontiac GTO. New inside. New outside. New wider Wide-Track. New undent bumper that's the same color as the car, but won't chip, peel or fade. And undents itself. 13 new exterior colors. New disappearing windshield wipers. New twin-scooped hood. New extra-cost hideaway headlights. New padded dash with wood-grain styled paneling. New 350-hp Quadra-Power 400. New carburetor air preheater. New front seat shoulder belts. And you can order a 360-hp 400 or the 360-hp Ram Air that turns those hood scoops into the real thing. Hardtop or convertible. The Great One is back. Aren't you glad you waited? (Only don't wait too long.)

Color pictures, specs and decals are yours for 30¢ (50¢ outside U.S.A.) to: '68 Wide-Tracks, P.O. Box 888G, 196 Wide-Track Blvd., Pontiac, Michigan, 48056.

GM
MARK OF EXCELLENCE

If you think Wide-Tracking is just a slogan, you've never been behind the wheel of The Great One.

Slogans don't straighten curves. Or conquer hills with the ease of an Alpine tram. But then, not many cars do, either. Which is why our GTO is so reverently referred to as The Great One. Its ability in the aforementioned situations stems from a standard 400-cubic-inch, 4-barrel V-8. A 3-speed with Hurst shifter. And Fastrak, redline tires that adhere to the road like glue clings to your fingers.

However, The Great One didn't merit *Motor Trend* magazine's

"Car of the Year" accolade merely for its driving prowess. Its polished sheet metal is molded into the shape of tomorrow. And up front, the world's most fantastic bumper. So fantastic, you have to kick it to believe it.

So when you next read that Wide-Tracking in a GTO is great, don't shrug and turn the page. See your Pontiac dealer. Where test drives speak louder than words.

Wide-Track 1968 Pontiacs

Pontiac Firebird 400. Swinging variation on a Wide-Track theme.

The question was, what do we do to turn a Great Wide-Tracker into Pontiac's ultimate answer to the American road?

The answer was, build the Firebird 400. And build it with a 400-cubic-inch, 330-horsepower Pontiac V-8. The kind of engine that makes you wonder why they tunnel through mountains when it's so easy to go over them.

Then, equip the 400 with Wide-Track stance and very wide tires.

They hold the Firebird to an "S" curve the way a roller coaster holds to a hairpin.

Then, finish the Firebird off with an interior of bucket seats. Morrokide upholstery (it acts so much like leather, only a cow can tell for sure). And a Hurst for shifting away idle minutes. That is, if you can find any in a 400. Because about the only time they're likely to occur is when you close the garage door.

Wide-Track 1968 Pontiacs

Announcing Pontiac's new Ram Air II.

Pontiac Motor Division

It grooms 340 hp from 5400 rpm. Twists 445 lbs. ft. of torque at 3800 rpm. And breathes air through two hood scoops. And for Ram Air's moderate extra cost, we've also added a new high-lift cam. New forged aluminum pistons. New Armasteel crankshaft, new push rods and guides and dual high-rate valve springs. New freer breathing combustion chamber with 36% larger exhaust ports. New "tulip head" lightweight valves. Welcome, friends of the automobile.

Anxious for 5 color pictures, specs and decals of the Great Wide-Tracks? Don't be. Send 30¢ (50¢ outside U.S.A.) to: '68 Wide-Tracks, P.O. Box 888B, 196 Wide-Track Blvd., Pontiac, Michigan 48056.

We wouldn't expect you to buy a Grand Prix for its hidden antenna alone.   Obviously.

True, our hidden antenna is a Break Away. No one else has one. But then, no one else has a 118" wheelbase. Or a hood that stretches from here to Duesenberg.

What's under the hood is enough to get under a test pilot's skin. 350 hp in a 400-cubic-inch block. Or you can order 428 cubic inches with 370 or 390 hp.

The most exotic interior ever to stay below 20,000 feet is also in the offing.

In fact, we figure if Strato-bucket seats, squeeze-release doors and airplane-style instruments don't give you a charge, it's time to give up driving.

After all, driving is what G.P.'s all about.

Right beside you is the shifting end of a 3-speed, fully synchronized manual or an available, 4-speed, Hurst-armed box. Or you can order the champion marriage-saver of all time. A Turbo Hydra-matic that either runs through the gears no hands, or lets you shift for yourself like a man.

About that hidden antenna. Since we wouldn't expect you to buy a Wide-Track Grand Prix for it, we won't bother to tell you where it is. Maybe your Pontiac dealer will.

The year of the Great Pontiac Break Away.

All rise for The Judge.

The Judge. From Pontiac.

A new name. With a special brand of justice to discourage the so-called performance-minded competition.

Like a standard, 366-horse, 400-cubic-inch V-8 with Ram Air and a 4-barrel. Or a 370-horse, 400-cube Ram Air IV V-8, if you so order. Either way, those hood scoops function.

Like a fully synchronized, floor-mounted, 3-speed cogbox. A close-ratio 4-speed with Hurst shifter (yea!) and a 3-speed Turbo Hydra-matic (boo!) are also in the hopper, if you'd care to order same.

Like a 60" air foil, blackened grille, exposed headlamps, fiber glass belted tires (big and black), steel mag-type wheels, blue-red-yellow striping and Judge I.D. inside and out.

Like an Endura schnoz that regards chips, dings and scrapes as acts of treason.

Like Morrokide-covered buckets. And a no-nonsense instrument panel that fills you in. In detail.

Order a hood-mounted tach and power front disc brakes.

Our case rests. It's justice, man.

THE JUDGE

PONTIAC | GM

We'd like to put in a good word for hoods.

Why not? We've got the toughest looking in the business.

Take that sweep of metal on the '69 Pontiac Grand Prix. You won't find a longer stretch from Sing Sing to Alcatraz.

The two bulges on Firebird 400 and GTO are pretty unsubtle, too. They're air scoops. Functional when you order Ram Air.

Now, you can order a tach for each of these hoods. And they'll look tougher. But let's face it. No hood's complete without a persuader.

Pontiac has them.

Grand Prix's is a standard 350-horse, 400-cubic-inch V-8. Or specify a 370- or 390-horse 428-cube V-8.

Firebird 400 has a 330-horse, 400-cubic-inch V-8 standard. You get even more impressive statistics when you order the H.O. or Ram Air IV version.

GTO started it all. Remember? A 350-horse, 400-cubic-inch V-8 is standard. A 366-hp V-8 and a 370-hp Ram Air IV await your order.

Obviously, this is no year to go around bad-mouthing Pontiac's hoods.

GM
Pontiac Motor Division

Move over mountain. This is the way it's going to be.

The Humbler is here. Pontiac GTO. If the sight of it doesn't turn you on, the sound of it will.

Listen. It's a 400-cube V-8 speaking out through a new, low-restriction performance exhaust you can order. And if you'd like to be even more vocal, order the new 455-cube V-8 with automatic box. (Hill, lay low.) Or, for the big shooters, the ultimate: our 400-cube, 370-hp Ram Air IV. With a fully synched, Hurst-shifted, 3-speed cogbox. 4-speed if you so specify.

Curve, straighten out. The Humbler will take you in style. With new, firmer control shocks. New front and rear stabilizer bars. Big, wide fiberglass-belted boots.

The Humbler. This is the way it's going to be, baby.

Pontiac's New GTO

GM
MARK OF EXCELLENCE

(We take the fun of driving seriously.)

(We take the fun of driving seriously.)

The Humbler.

1970 Pontiac GTO. So dazzling we've thrown modesty to the wind and dubbed it "The Humbler."

Listen. You'll catch on. The basso burble comes from a new performance exhaust you can order.

Of course, pipes can't do it alone. Standard Humbler is a 400 V-8. But you can order a new 455 V-8. Or one of the Ram Air engines.

You can also specify the Hurst-stirred 4-speed, instead of the standard 3-speed.

About now, a lot of pseudo performers would like to slither off to a nice, quiet garage. Frankly, there's not a cozier place for them to eat their humble pie. And obviously dessert is served. The Humbler's here.

Pontiac Motor Division

3 individual color pictures of Pontiac performance cars, specs, book jackets and decals are yours for 40¢ (60¢ outside U.S.A.). Write to: '70 Wide-Tracks, P.O. Box 888, 196 Wide-Track Blvd., Pontiac, Mich. 48056.

(We take the fun of driving seriously.)

Gauges that gauge, spoilers that spoil, and scoops that scoop.

What's this? Detroit pushing functional styling? Wouldn't you know who. Pontiac.

We decided to give our designers and engineers their heads. And what they came up with is styling that works. Aerodynamically. In four totally new Firebirds. Two of which you just might find particularly stirring.

Firebird Formula 400 (the blue beauty shown left). We asked ourselves how many passengers we might seat comfortably. The answer was four. So Formula 400 has bucket seats front and rear.

Then, we raised the drive line tunnel between the seats to get more room for spring travel. And the result is a decided lack of the typical sports car jolts.

Formula 400 also has a bigger stabilizer bar up front. A brand-new stabilizer bar in the rear. And standard front disc brakes. For those roads that feature curves. The fastest variable-ratio power steering around is available for such conditions, too.

The standard 330-hp, 400-cubic-inch V-8 should be enough for about anyone. Just in case somebody disagrees, however, there's a 400 Ram Air V-8 you can order.

Should you do so, the scoops perched on that fiberglass hood will scoop. Really scoop. Take a glance at the available full complement of honest-to-gosh gauges if you doubt us.

Just remember who told whom about functional styling.

Firebird Trans Am (the one shown right that isn't blue). Ah, what a little road testing can do. What it can do is help you develop a front air dam and side air extractors that put a 50-lb. downward pressure on the front end. At turnpike speeds, it can show you how effective air dams are at the wheel wells. It can lead you into developing a rear spoiler that puts 50 lbs. of pressure on the rear end. Also at turnpike speeds.

And it can convince you that a shaker hood with a rear-facing inlet is effective for providing air to a 345-hp, 400-cubic-inch Ram Air V-8.

It can also tell you how it all works with the Hurst-shifted wide- or close-ratio 4-speed transmission you can order.

Now you know why Trans Am is our most sophisticated Firebird. In fact, the only thing that doesn't function is the unsubtle stripe running the length of the car. But maybe it does something for you.

GM

Pontiac Motor Division

New, even for Pontiac.

Blacked-out grille.
Body stripes.
3-speed floor shift.
Sport mirrors.
Carpeting.
Custom Sport steering wheel.

That's how Pontiac builds an economy car.

The 1972 Ventura II Sprint. OK, it's a little economy car with California cosmetics. (Bucket seats and even a sun-roof are available.) But beneath the sporty looks there's a lot about Sprint that'll make a car enthusiast enthusiastic.

A six of another stripe. Sprint is powered by a 6-cylinder engine that's been around long enough to have the bugs worked out. It's economical. Easy to work on. And we think it's the best production six on the road. Here's why:

It has a fully counterweighted 7-main-bearing crank. It has overhead valves with an aircraft-type operating system. It has a precision-built cast block with thin walls for high-velocity coolant flow. It has a chrome alloy head and modified-wedge combustion chambers.

So, even with an economical six, Sprint comes on like a Pontiac. Of course, if you're still not convinced on sixes, there's a 307-CID V-8 you can order. (On Sprints built in California, the available V-8 has 350 cubic inches.)

The same credentials that apply to the six apply to the eights. They're rugged. Uncomplicated. Easy to work on. And face it, they do give the Sprint a bit more swagger.

Well-suspended animation. No matter how great the performance, it's worthless if it can't be handled. So the Sprint is designed to respond. Corner. And stop. With authority.

The suspension is computer-selected, with independent front coils and rear leafs. If you'd like it firmer, there's a heavy-duty suspension package you can order.

The brakes are big no-drag drums. Front discs are available.

The tires are road-gripping E78 whitewalls mounted on wide 14 x 6 wheels.

Order power steering on the Sprint and you'll get variable-ratio power steering. It's quick and precise. It keeps turning faster as you keep turning farther. 2.3 turns, lock to lock.

The class of its class. Stack Ventura II Sprint up against the other cars in its class, and you'll see how much it offers the enthusiast. It's a tough, confident little road car. With a low initial price, and low upkeep costs.

But no enthusiast ever got sold on a car by reading about it. So get down to your Pontiac dealer's and get sold on the Sprint. By driving it.

Ventura II Sprint...a cut above.
Buckle up for safety.

GTO is built for driving. So are the available buckets. They're firm. Contoured. Comfortable.

Pontiac's Radial Tuned Suspension. Worth ordering. FR78-14 steel-belted radials. Front and rear bars. Firmer shocks. Computer-selected springs.

A new shaker hood scoops cold, dense air. For more performance.

Pontiac's new 350 4-bbl. V-8 is standard. It won't disappoint you.

With GTO, you stir from the floor. 3 speeds standard. 4 available.

The Wide-Track people have a way with cars.

Announcing Pontiac's new GTO. This tough little compact didn't just inherit its great name. It earned it.

MOTOR TREND: OCTOBER '73. NOT QUITE THE BEAST LIKE THE GTO'S FROM THE SIXTIES, THIS VENTURA-BASED VERSION WAS STILL SOMETHING TO RECKON WITH.

Chapter Five
Studebaker Corporation

For you action lovers...

THE LARK DAYTONA

America's new action car

Bold...bucket-seated...accelerating from 0 to 60 in less than 10 seconds—that's the glamorous new '62 Lark Daytona. Especially created for today's action-loving young Americans, the Lark Daytona combines an optional 4-speed gearbox, nimble 109 inch wheelbase, and up to 225 HP—tames traffic, Thruway, or Rally route with equal ease.

Stop in at your nearest Studebaker dealer for a test-drive in either the Lark Daytona Hardtop or Convertible. We think you'll like the handy between-seat console, wood-grained dash, sports type instrumentation, the hardtop's unique optional Skytop sunroof. Then touch your foot to the accelerator...ask yourself if you've ever seen so much car for even $1000 more.

new '62 LARK

ENDURANCE-BUILT BY STUDEBAKER

See all eight new '62 Lark models today at your Studebaker dealer

STUDEBAKER

invites your inspection

of a distinctive new family sports classic

The Gran Turismo
Hawk

designed and made in the meticulous tradition of

the great European road cars and offering

the comforts and conveniences

preferred by the discerning

American motorist

- *The embodiment of roadability and driving ease — from the gleaming expanse of hood through the smallest hand-crafted detail*
- *Full 120" wheelbase; Thunderbolt V-8 engine • Finned-drum brakes; anti-sway bar; floor-mounted 4-speed gear box**
- *European style walnut grained concave control panel with full sports type instrumentation; optional tachometer*
- *True Gran Turismo interiors: full five-passenger capacity; sports car type bucket seats forward, let-down arm rest in rear*
- *Luxurious upholstery, trim and appointments • All popular power and automatic options, of course.*
  *Optional

TAKE AN ACTION RIDE
IN AMERICA'S NEW ACTION CAR,
THE LARK DAYTONA

Here's where it begins, facing a wood-grained sports-type instrument panel. *Feel the fit of pedals on feet, the properly raked wheel for real driving.* *Settle deep into the bucket seat and get ready.*

Enjoy the smooth surge of the Lark Daytona's take-off roll...you move! Shift crisply through... *...gears with a solid four-speed box*. Streak swiftly down on the sands powered on your way* *...by 225 HP of the four-barrel carburetor* Studebaker V-8. Faster and faster you go.*

Now, call a halt with huge finned brake drums. *Deceleration is dramatic. You stop surely, with control...* *...gently. It's easy. Fun. Handsome. Try it.*

*OPTIONAL   **SEE YOUR STUDEBAKER DEALER!**

MOTOR TREND: DECEMBER '61. THE THUNDERBOLT MENTIONED COULD BE THE 289 FOUR-BARREL THAT PRODUCED 225 HP.

MOTOR TREND: DECEMBER '61

Introducing America's Most Advanced Automobile

"You are looking at a new take-off point for the American Automobile. It is the Avanti by Studebaker. It is a prestige car, a fast car, a safe car, and certainly the most advanced car produced in America today."

SHERWOOD H. EGBERT, PRESIDENT, STUDEBAKER CORPORATION

Avanti by Studebaker

The Avanti is a car to please the senses. It is graceful to the eye and exhilarating to the spirit. It looks different and is different. It combines design and engineering features as no other American car does. Admittedly this is a car for the discriminating. It is intended to please individuals desiring an advanced automobile with exceptional performance and great distinction.

HERE ARE BUT SOME OF THE AVANTI'S EXCITING FEATURES:

Aerodynamic wedge design.

Comfortable bucket seats for four adults.

Disc brakes up front. First American passenger car to use them. Full power assist all four wheels.

Vanity case with illuminated mirror built into glove locker.

*New, unique automatic "Power-shift" transmission—acts as a fully automatic or can be shifted up or down.

Choice of high-performance manual transmissions—3 and 4* speed.

Complete instrumentation with tachometer and manifold pressure gauge.

Aircraft type red instrument illumination for superior night vision.

Aircraft type overhead controls for lights and fan.

Cockpit type heater-defroster controls on a console-mounted "throttle" quadrant.

Built-in padded steel safety bar over passenger compartment.

Safety-padded interior.

High performance Jet-thrust V8—4 bbl. carburetor. *Paxton supercharger for extraordinary performance.

Large luggage-contoured trunk.

Access panel connects car interior to trunk.

*Power steering—exceptionally fast—only three turns full right to full left.

Performance-matched axle ratios available.

Limited slip differential. (Twin Traction)

Safety cone door locks will not fly open even under great stress.

Would you like to have an Avanti built for you? Visit your Studebaker Dealer. He is taking orders on a priority basis.

*Optional

"Indy" 500 winner Rodger Ward (left) shows his Avanti to friends.

"Indy" 500 Winner, Rodger Ward, Becomes World's First Avanti Owner

We are proud that Rodger Ward is the first Studebaker Avanti owner, for this is a car built not only for knowledgeable drivers, but for all admirers of exceptional automobiles.

As such, every Avanti will be carefully inspected through every phase of manufacture and road tested before shipment from the factory.

Not only is Avanti performance outstanding (0-60 in 6.7 seconds), but its handling characteristics are outstanding too. Steering is a little over three turns lock to lock, and the entire car is taut and precise. Its deceleration is as dramatic as its acceleration. Caliper-type discs up front and finned Bendix drums at the rear provide a superb braking system.

And the Avanti seats four comfortably in an elegant tastefully appointed interior. Bolstered bucket seats, anatomically designed, help make long distance cruising effortless. Write for an illustrated brochure in color that gives you all the details. The address is Studebaker Corporation, 635 South Main St., South Bend 27, Indiana.

Avanti by Studebaker
America's Most Advanced Automobile

HOLIDAY: JUNE '62. THE TIMELESS BEAUTY OF THE RAYMOND LOEWY-DESIGNED AVANTI.

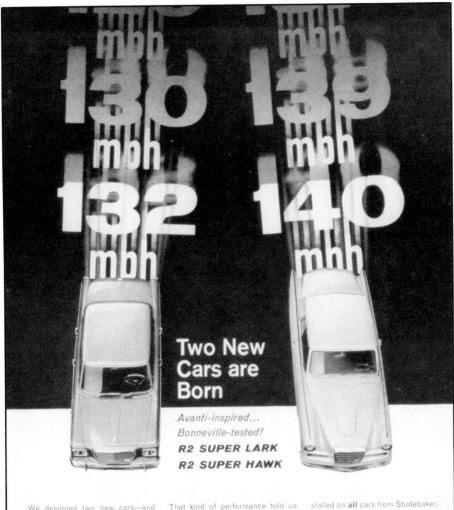

MOTOR TREND: MAY '63. GOING 140 MPH IS TOUGH TO BEAT IN ANYONE'S BOOK.

MOTOR TREND: JUNE '63

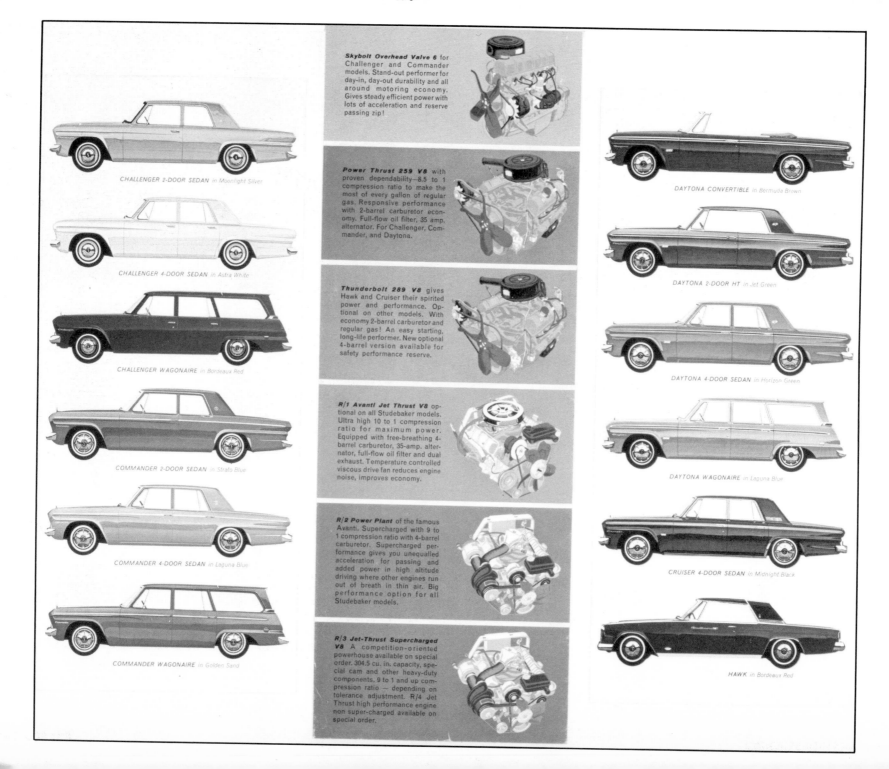

CHALLENGER 2-DOOR SEDAN in Moonlight Silver

CHALLENGER 4-DOOR SEDAN in Astra White

CHALLENGER WAGONAIRE in Bordeaux Red

COMMANDER 2-DOOR SEDAN in Strato Blue

COMMANDER 4-DOOR SEDAN in Laguna Blue

COMMANDER WAGONAIRE in Golden Sand

Skybolt Overhead Valve 6 for Challenger and Commander models. Stand-out performer for day-in, day-out durability and all around motoring economy. Gives steady efficient power with lots of acceleration and reserve passing zip!

Power Thrust 259 V8 with proven dependability—8.5 to 1 compression ratio to make the most of every gallon of regular gas. Responsive performance with 2-barrel carburetor economy. Full-flow oil filter, 35 amp. alternator. For Challenger, Commander, and Daytona.

Thunderbolt 289 V8 gives Hawk and Cruiser their spirited power and performance. Optional on other models. With economy 2-barrel carburetor and regular gas! An easy starting, long-life performer. New optional 4-barrel version available for safety performance reserve.

R/1 Avanti Jet Thrust V8 optional on all Studebaker models. Ultra high 10 to 1 compression ratio for maximum power. Equipped with free-breathing 4-barrel carburetor, 35-amp. alternator, full-flow oil filter and dual exhaust. Temperature controlled viscous drive fan reduces engine noise, improves economy.

R/2 Power Plant of the famous Avanti. Supercharged with 9 to 1 compression ratio with 4-barrel carburetor. Supercharged performance gives you unequalled acceleration for passing and added power in high altitude driving where other engines run out of breath in thin air. Big performance option for all Studebaker models.

R/3 Jet-Thrust Supercharged V8 A competition-oriented powerhouse available on special order. 304.5 cu. in. capacity, special cam and other heavy-duty components. 9 to 1 and up compression ratio — depending on tolerance adjustment. R/4 Jet Thrust high performance engine non super-charged available on special order.

DAYTONA CONVERTIBLE in Bermuda Brown

DAYTONA 2-DOOR HT in Jet Green

DAYTONA 4-DOOR SEDAN in Horizon Green

DAYTONA WAGONAIRE in Laguna Blue

CRUISER 4-DOOR SEDAN in Midnight Black

HAWK in Bordeaux Red

THE POWER IS THE STORY...

of the '64 Studebakers

Take USAC's word for it—they clocked a fleet of sizzling '64 Studes at Bonneville. Our smallest power plant, the economy Six, flicked through the USAC traps for an average two-way speed of 102.77 mph in the flying mile. Our soft-top Daytona, with an optional blown Avanti R-3 mill under the hood, shot through at 153.48 mph.

Studebaker filled whole pages in the USAC record books at this '64 session. Not just so you can take off like the kangaroo with a hotfoot. Mostly it's for the thrill of holding legal speeds at half throttle. It's also insurance against the day when you're two-thirds past a truck and somebody barrels over a hilltop at you, astride the white line.

You can pick a Studebaker for looks, or solid handling, or big room, or giant economy—but your real satisfaction is down there in the engine room. Go get a free sample of Studebaker's '64 power, at your nearest dealer's.

different by design

Studebaker
AUTOMOTIVE SALES CORPORATION

Open-top Wagonaire   Luxury 'Cruiser'   Power-packed Hawk

UNITED STATES AUTO CLUB
Certified and sanctioned by the United States Auto Club

Record-breaking Daytona

Avanti II SPECIFICATIONS

Overall length	192.5
Overall width	70.4"
Overall height	54.0"
Wheelbase	109.0
Shipping Weight	3.181
Turning Diameter (curb to curb)	37.5"
Headroom-front-rear	36"-33.625
Legroom-front-rear	47"-36.25
Hiproom-front-rear	49.5"-47.5
Shoulder-room-front-rear	52.5-51.5

ENGINE

Bore and stroke	4.00 x 3.25
Piston displacement	327
Compression ratio	10.5 : 1
Horsepower	300 @ 5000
Torque	360 @ 3200

STANDARD EQUIPMENT

Air Conditioning
Automatic Floor Transmission or —
Four Speed in Floor
Heater & Defroster
Adjustomatic Tilt Steering Wheel
Power Steering
Push Button Radio
Seat Belts Front & Rear
Sun Band Windshield Front & Rear
Tinted Side Windows
Firestone 500 Nylon White Walls
7.75 x 15
Twin Traction Limited-Slip Differential
Electric Windows
Power Disc Brakes
Windshield Washers
Rear View Mirror—Non Glare
Interior Decorator Fabrics
Hand Craft Tool Pouch & Kit
4-Way "SOS" Emergency Flasher
Heavy Duty Springs Front & Rear

Wheel Disc—Hub Caps
Delcotron 12 Volt Alternator
Back-up Lights
Brakes: Front Caliper—Rear Finned
Drums
Bucket Seats
Stabilizer, Front & Rear
Steering Wheel—Wood Grained Tenite
Padded Sun Visors
Tachometer
Vanity Tray—Instrument Board
with Lamp and Mirror
Console Between Bucket Seats
Cigar Lighter
Electric Clock
Coat Hooks
Directional Signals
Chrome Drip Moldings
Four Barrel Carburetor
Viscous Drive 5-Blade Fan
Gas Filter in Line
Gas Line Drain

Vacuum Pressure Gauge
Padded Instrument Board
Wood Grained Instrument Panel
Internal Trunk Release
Courtesy Lights
2 Dome & One Instrument Board
Trunk Compartment Light
Moldings, Windshield & Rear
Window Stainless Steel
Full Flow Oil Filter
Rear Axle Radius Rods
Rear Axle Heavy Duty
Roll Bar, Safety Padded
Shock Absorbers, Heavy Duty
Adjustable Front & Rear
Speedometer—140 miles per hour
Electric Windshield Wipers, two-speed
Dual Exhaust System and Resonators
21 Gallon Fuel Tank
Safety Padded Interior
Specifications subject to change

Avanti MOTOR CORPORATION
765 So. Lafayette Blvd.
South Bend, Ind. 46623

"Some people in South Bend, Indiana, still think Nathan Altman is crazy. Yet, he has resurrected a ghost car, a loser before its death, and turned it into one of the world's most desirable automobiles in the face of odds which even the big Detroit auto makers wouldn't buck."

Esquire Magazine, April 1970

Crazy? Maybe so! □ Desirable? Without a doubt! □ Unbelievable? Drive it, and you'll never go back to your present car. □ But don't take our word for it. □ Drop us a line and we'll send you a reprint of the Esquire story. □ Avanti II . . . more than a car, a love affair!

Avanti II
"Once in a lifetime"

SPECIFICATIONS*

Overall Length	197.5"
Overall Width	70.4"
Overall Height	54.0"
Wheelbase	109.0"
Shipping Weight	3.250
Turning Diameter (curb to curb)	37.5"
Headroom/front-rear	36"-34.5"
Legroom/front-rear	47"-36.25"
Hiproom/front-rear	49.5"-47.5"
Shoulder-room/front-rear	52.5"-51.5"
Bore & Stroke	4.126 x 3.75
Piston Displacement	400 cu. inch
Compression Ratio	8.5-1
Horsepower	245 @ 4400
Torque 400 cu. inch	390 @ 2400

Specifications subject to change without notice.

AVANTI MOTOR CORPORATION   765 S. Lafayette • South Bend, Indiana   AC 219 287-1836

1966 AUTO SHOW PROGRAM. EVEN THOUGH AVANTI II WAS NOT MADE BY STUDEBAKER, IT'S INCLUDED FOR YOUR INTEREST.

1973 AUTO SHOW PROGRAM

More Great Reading

American Car Spotter's Guide 1966-1980. Giant pictorial source with over 3,600 illus., 432 pages, softbound.

Chrysler and Imperial: The Postwar Years. Year-by-year account through 1976 of this fascinating story. 216 pages, 488 photos.

Oldsmobile: The Postwar Years. 280 fine illustrations help tell this exciting story through 1980. 152 pages.

Shelby's Wildlife: The Cobras and Mustangs. Complete, exciting story of the 260, 289, 427 and Daytona Cobras plus Shelby Mustangs. 224 pages, nearly 200 photos.

Lincoln and Continental: The Postwar Years. Interesting historical information through 1980. 152 pages, 223 illustrations.

Chevy Super Sports 1961-1976. Exciting story of these hot cars with complete specs and data. 178 pages, 198 illus., softbound.

Ferraris For The Road. Provides lavish pictorial coverage of Ferrari's production models. In the Survivors Series. 126 pages, 269 photos, many in color.

Illustrated Ferrari Buyer's Guide. Features all street production models 1954 through 1980. 169 pages, over 230 photos, softbound.

Automotive Fuel Injection Systems: A Technical Guide. Thorough analysis and description of current gas-engine fuel injection technology. 173 illus., 182 pages, softbound.

Buick: The Postwar Years. Comprehensive history of a styling and engineering leader. 166 pages, 157 photos.

The Art & Science of Grand Prix Driving. Incisive look at F1 cars and techniques by world driving champion Niki Lauda. 245 pages, 158 photos, 23 in color.

The Ford Agency: A Pictorial History. The complete story of Ford's dealer network. 131 pages, 260 great period photos, softbound.

Chevy Spotter's Guide 1920-1980. Nearly 1,200 illus. of Chevrolet cars and trucks for the enthusiast. 133 pages, softbound.

Ford Spotter's Guide 1920-1980. A great 136-page reference of Ford autos and trucks. Over 1,100 illus., softbound.

American Car Spotter's Guide 1940-1965. (Revised). Greatly enlarged edition—almost 3,000 illus., 358 pages, softbound.

Porsches For The Road. Includes photo essays on 12 models. In the Survivors Series. 128 pages, 250 illus., 125 in color.

The Thunderbird Story: Personal Luxury. Full story of first 26 years is told with 275 exquisite photos, 23 in beautiful color. 144 large-format pages.

My Years With Ferrari. Candid and articulate telling of World Champion Niki Lauda's ascendancy to the top of the racing world. 54 pages of color and black & white photos, 237 pages.

Make Money Owning Your Car. Down-to-earth analysis on beating high depreciation and interest costs of car ownership. 179 pages, 96 photos.

Corvair Affair. The complete story of the Corvair including styling, mechanicals and the Nader connection. 176 pages, over 140 great illus.

The Big "Little GTO" Book. All of these Great Ones by Pontiac are covered—1965-1974. Over 150 great photos, 235 pages.

Muscle Car Mania: An Advertising Collection. 250 of those great promotional ads for 1964 through 1974 muscle cars. Softbound, 176 pages.

The Cobra Story. Autobiography of Carroll Shelby and Cobra production & racing history through 1965. 272 pages, 60 photos.

Auto Restoration From Junker To Jewel. Illustrated guide to restoring old cars. 232 pages, 289 illustrations, softbound.

American Car Spotter's Guide 1920-1939. Shows models of 217 makes. 290 pages, 2,607 illus., softbound.

Pontiac: The Postwar Years: One of America's most interesting makes is covered in this factual story. 205 pages, 222 photos.

Specification Book for U.S. Cars 1930-1969. Information on 250 makes including Canadian. 400 pages, softbound.

Studebaker: The Postwar Years. Interesting history includes the company's downhill slide and bounce back from apparent defeat. 192 pages, 309 photos.